Fire™ Tablets

FOR

DUMMIES®

A Wiley Brand

by Nancy Muir

Fire™ Tablets For Dummies®

Published by: **John Wiley & Sons, Inc.,** 111 River Street, Hoboken, NJ 07030-5774, www.wiley.com

Copyright © 2015 by John Wiley & Sons, Inc., Hoboken, New Jersey

Published simultaneously in Canada

For general information on our other products and services, please contact our Customer Care Department within the U.S. at 877-762-2974, outside the U.S. at 317-572-3993, or fax 317-572-4002. For technical support, please visit www.wiley.com/techsupport.

Wiley publishes in a variety of print and electronic formats and by print-on-demand. Some material included with standard print versions of this book may not be included in e-books or in print-on-demand. If this book refers to media such as a CD or DVD that is not included in the version you purchased, you may download this material at http://booksupport.wiley.com. For more information about Wiley products, visit www.wiley.com.

Library of Congress Control Number: 2014951012

ISBN 978-1-119-00825-5 (pbk); ISBN 978-1-119-00827-9 (ebk); ISBN 978-1-119-00826-2 (ebk)

Manufactured in the United States of America

10 9 8 7 6 5 4 3 2 1

Contents at a Glance

Table of Contents

Introduction

Amazon's Fire tablets provide a very affordable way to get at all kinds of media, from music and videos to books and colorful magazines. Any of the four tablet models also allow you to browse the Internet, connect to your Facebook account, make video calls via Skype, take photos, check your email, and read documents. The portability of both the 6- and 7-inch models makes them incredibly useful for people on the go. The 8.9-inch model is still pretty darn portable, and adds several features that are useful to those who want the most feature-rich tablet experience from Amazon.

In this book, I introduce you to all the cool Fire tablet features, providing tips and advice for getting the most out of these ingenious little devices. I help you find your way around the attractive and easy-to-use interface, provide advice about getting the most out of the Amazon Cloud Drive for storing and managing content, and even recommend some neat apps that make your Fire tablet more functional and fun. Finally, a complete chapter on using a Fire tablet to connect with and protect your family shows you features that integrate into your household.

About This Book

"If Fire tablets are so easy to use, why do I need a book?" you may be asking yourself. When I first sat down with the latest Fire tablets, it took about two weeks of poking around to find settings, features, and ways to buy and locate my content and apps. When was the last time you had two weeks to spare? I've spent the time so that you can quickly and easily get the hang of all the Fire tablet features and discover a few tricks I bet your friends won't uncover for quite a while.

This book uses certain conventions that are helpful to understand, including

- ✔ Text that you're meant to type just as it appears in the book is **bold**. The exception is when you're working through a step list: Because each step is bold, the text to type is not bold.

- ✔ Web addresses appear in `monofont`. If you're reading a digital version of this book on a device connected to the Internet, note that you can click or tap the web address to visit that website, like this: `www.dummies.com`.

This book covers many of the features in the original Kindle Fire, released in 2011, as well as Kindle Fire HD, released in 2012, and Kindle Fire HDX, which appeared in 2013. Though this book is focused on the latest Fire tablet models released in 2014, whichever Fire model you own, you should find lots of advice and answers in this book.

Foolish Assumptions

You may have opted for a tablet to watch movies and read books on the run. You might think it's a good way to browse business documents and check email on your next plane trip. You might have one or more computers and be very computer savvy, or you might hate computers and figure that a Fire tablet gives you all the computing power you need to browse the Internet and read ebooks. Perhaps you see the Fire HD Kids Edition tablet as a great way to direct and monitor your child's computer learning experience.

Fire users come in all types. I don't assume in this book that you're a computer whiz, but I do assume that you have a passing understanding of how to copy a file and plug in a USB cable. I'm guessing you've browsed the Internet at least a few times and heard of Wi-Fi, which is what you use to go online with a Fire tablet (unless you purchased the LTE version, which uses a cellular connection just like your phone). Other than that, you don't need a lot of technical background to get the most out of this book.

Icons Used in This Book

Icons are little pictures in the margin of this book that alert you to special types of advice or information, including

There aren't too many ways you can get in trouble with the Fire tablets, but in those few situations where some action might be irreversible, I include warnings so you can avoid any pitfalls.

When you see this icon, you'll know that I'm emphasizing important information for you to keep in mind as you use a feature.

These short words of advice draw your attention to faster, easier, or alternative ways of getting things done with Fire tablets.

Beyond the Book

There is extra online content about Fire tablets that goes beyond the book itself. Go online to take advantage of these features:

- ✔ **Cheat Sheet** (www.dummies.com/cheatsheet/firetablets)**:** The Cheat Sheet for this book includes a table of information about all the Quick Settings available to you, including settings to adjust screen brightness and the new Mayday online support button.

- ✔ **Dummies.com online articles:** The parts pages of this book provide links to articles on Dummies.com that extend the content covered in the book. The articles appear on the book's Extras page at www.dummies.com/extras/firetablets. Topics include staying safe online, getting more out of OfficeSuite, and ten great apps for kids.

- ✔ **Updates:** Here's where you can find updates in case the book changes substantially: www.dummies.com/extras/firetablets.

Where to Go from Here

Time to get that Fire out of its box, set it up, and get going with all the fun, entertaining things it makes available to you. Have fun!

Part I
Getting Started with Fire Tablets

getting started
with

Fire Tablets

In this part . . .

✔ Take a look at your Fire tablet.

✔ Turn it on and set it up for first use.

✔ Read about how to use the touchscreen.

✔ Set up profiles for yourself and your children.

1

Getting an Overview of Fire Tablets

In This Chapter

▶ Discovering what's new in the latest Fire tablets

▶ Comparing Fire tablets to the competition

▶ Surveying all of the Fire tablet's features

*Y*our Fire tablet isn't just an ereader. It's a handheld computer with a touchscreen and an onscreen keyboard for providing input, and with apps that allow you to play games, read ebooks, check email, browse the web, watch movies, listen to music, and more.

Amazon, the giant online retailer, just happens to have access to more content (music, movies, audio books, and so on) than just about anybody on the planet. So, when an Amazon tablet debuted a few years ago, and as Amazon stacked up media partnerships with the likes of Fox and PBS, the Kindle Fire tablet was seen as the first real challenge to Apple's iPad.

Now, in its fourth generation and rebranded as simply Fire, these four tablet models offer very nice improvements at the right price and feature mix for many people, while offering the key to that treasure chest of content that Amazon has been wise enough to amass.

In this chapter, you get an overview of the four Fire tablets: how they compare to competing devices and what their key features are. Subsequent chapters delve into how to use all those features in detail.

Checking Out the Four Fire Tablet Models

In 2014, Amazon introduced four Fire tablet models that offer slightly different features and pricing, including a Fire HD Kids edition, which comes in a 6-inch or 7-inch display.

Essentially, the 8.9-inch Fire tablet sports a faster processor, higher resolution screen, higher-end cameras, the most current Wi-Fi standard, and Dolby Atmos multidimensional sound (which means when wearing headphones you hear sounds from multiple locations, as you might in a movie theater).

In addition, the Kids edition has a rugged casing, two-year replacement warranty, robust parental controls, and a free year of access to Amazon's FreeTime Unlimited with age-appropriate content.

Other than these major differences, all the models include

- Unlimited Amazon Cloud storage for photos taken with your Fire model or content bought from Amazon.
- An integrated app to work with Microsoft Office documents.
- A free month of Amazon Prime, which provides free two-day shipping for many Amazon products, as well as access to a treasure trove of free products (video, music, and books).
- X-Ray provides background information about artists, movies, musicians, and more when you're looking up or playing content.

Table 1-1 helps you make sense of the differences among the various models.

Tablet 1-1	Fire Model Comparison			
Feature	*Fire 8.9"*	*Fire 7"*	*Fire 6"*	*Fire HD Kids Edition*
Quad-core 2.5 GHz processor	X			
Quad-core 1.5 GHz processor		X	X	X
1280 x 800 screen resolution		X	X	X
2560 x 1600 resolution	X			
Wi-Fi	Dual band, dual antenna	Single-band	Single-band	Single-band
Support for 802.11 ac Wi-Fi	X			
Dolby Audio		X	X	X
Dolby ATMOS	X			
4G model available	X			
Front-facing VGA camera		X	X	X

Feature	Fire 8.9"	Fire 7"	Fire 6"	Fire HD Kids Edition
Front-facing HD camera	X			
2MP rear camera		X	X	X
8MP rear camera	X			
Unlimited Amazon Cloud storage	X	X	X	X
Mayday live help	X			
Battery	12 hours	8 hours	8 hours	8 hours
Storage	16, 32, 64 GB	8 or 16 GB	8 or 16 GB	8 GB
Two-year Worry-Free Warranty				X
Kid-proof case				X
Accelerator/ gyroscope	X	X	X	X
Price starting at	$379	$139	$99	$149
Fire keyboard	X			
Firefly	X			
Dynamic Light Control	X			
One year of free FreeTime				X

In addition to these four models, Amazon offers the 2013 Fire HDX 7-inch tablet for $179. This is essentially last year's model, but it includes the Mayday help feature, a 2.2 GHz processor, and 1920 x 1200 display resolution, which is better than the newer 6- and 7-inch Fire models for not much more money.

If you prefer working with your Fire tablet on a stand rather than holding it in your hands, check out Meb's Kitchenwares (`http://www.mebskitchenwares.com/accessories.html`) to view their lovely handmade wooden tablet stand. It's portable, handcrafted from cherry wood, and at only $70 is a beautiful piece of furniture for your Fire tablet. Note it works best with the larger versions of the tablet and works in both portrait and landscape orientations.

What's New in the Latest Fire Tablets

Fire tablets with their new operating system, Fire OS 4.1.1, bring several new or improved features to the table:

- **Firefly:** A feature that was announced as "coming soon" at the time of this writing, Firefly is essentially a text-recognition app that allows 8.9-inch Fire tablets to identify text on movie posters, music albums, and so on. Firefly finds matches for the movie, music, or whatever in Amazon's huge online store. See Chapter 3 for more about Firefly. Updates will be posted at www.dummies.com/extras/firetablets.

- **Profiles:** You can create profiles for different people using your tablet so each has his own settings and content. This feature is like providing unique tablets for all the people in your family, including kids. See Chapter 5 for information about setting up profiles.

- **Family Library:** This new feature has also been announced but isn't yet available for Fire tablets as of this writing. Family Library allows you to link accounts to share content among a group or family members without sharing a tablet. See Chapter 5 for details about Family Library. Updates will be posted at www.dummies.com/extras/firetablets.

- **ASAP:** ASAP stands for Advanced Streaming and Prediction. Essentially, this feature allows your tablet to anticipate content you might want to watch, like your favorite TV show, and pre-load it for faster streaming. You don't have to do a thing to use this feature; just know it's working for you.

- **WPS Office:** Amazon made a change in the latest Fire tablets from OfficeSuite to WPS Office. WPS Office is more integrated into Fire and allows you to create, open, and work with Word, Excel, and PowerPoint files as well as a few other file formats. The working experience with documents is somehow more intuitive and simpler than in OfficeSuite. See Chapter 12 for more details about working with WPS Office.

- **Fire keyboard:** For the 8.9-inch model only, you can buy a keyboard accessory that attaches to your Fire tablet, making it possible to work on it comfortably as well as using it to view or listen to content like books, music, and videos.

- **Support for 802.11 ac Wi-Fi standard:** The 8.9-inch Fire has added support for the latest Wi-Fi standard, 802.11 ac. This makes your connection to Wi-Fi networks that much faster.

- **Second Screen:** This feature allows you to "fling" content from Amazon Cloud to your television. This causes the content to stream to the TV so that your Fire tablet is freed up (so you can do other things with it while watching your TV). You can even explore X-Ray information about the content on your tablet while it plays on your TV. Chapter 10 tells you how to set up and use Second Screen.

- ✔ **FreeTime Unlimited:** This feature, which comes free for one year with the latest Kids Edition Fire tablet, lets you create a unique environment by limiting what content and apps they can use. When you turn on FreeTime, your kids see only the content you've given them permission to use, and it's all shown against a kid-friendly graphical background. See Chapter 5 for more about FreeTime.

- ✔ **Integrated Goodreads:** This service is like a social network for readers. Goodreads was available as an app in previous Amazon tablets, but with the latest models this feature is more integrated. Goodreads allows you to track and share what you're reading and get access to reviews and recommendations from other readers via your Facebook and Twitter accounts.

- ✔ **SmartSuspend:** This is a battery setting that, when turned on in Power Management Settings, turns off your wireless connection when you're not using your Fire tablet. You can even set up a schedule for SmartSuspend to kick in. See Chapter 4 for the details on these settings.

- ✔ **Dynamic Light Control (DLC):** This feature, only available on the 8.9-inch Fire model, modifies your screen when reading ebooks to match ambient light. DLC produces a more paperlike background.

Key Features of Fire Tablets

Every Fire tablet has all the things most people want from a tablet packed into an easy-to-hold package: email, web browsing, players for video and music content, built-in calendar and contacts apps, an ereader, a great online content store, access to tens of thousands of Android apps, and so on. In the following sections, you get to explore some of these useful features.

Storage on Earth and in the Cloud

Fire tablet offers 8GB of storage in its 6- and 7-inch models, and 16GB, 32GB, or 64GB in the 8.9-inch models. Any storage amount will probably work just fine for you because when you own a Fire tablet, you get free, unlimited Amazon Cloud Drive storage for all digital content purchased from Amazon (but not content that you copy onto your Fire tablet from your computer by connecting a micro USB cable). This means that books, movies, music, and apps are held online for you to stream or download at any time you have access to Wi-Fi, instead of being stored on your Fire tablet.

This Amazon Cloud Drive storage means that you don't use up your Fire tablet memory. With the latest Fire tablets, you get unlimited Amazon Cloud storage for photos you take with the tablets and content you buy from Amazon.

As long as you have a Wi-Fi connection, you can stream content from Amazon Cloud at any time. If you'll be away from a connection, download an item (such as an episode of your favorite TV show), watch it, and then remove it from your device the next time you're within range of a Wi-Fi network. The content is still available in the Cloud: You can download that content again or stream it anytime you like.

If you want to go whole hog into your Fire tablet, you can opt for the highest memory device, the 64GB 8.9-inch Fire tablet 4G LTE Wireless version of the device. Just be aware that 4G devices come with the added cost of an AT&T or Verizon data plan.

App appeal

Your Fire tablet is generally easy to use, with a simple, Android-based touch-screen interface. Its primary focus is on consuming media — and consuming media is what Amazon is all about. Fire tablet also offers its own Silk browser; an email client; clock, calendar and contact apps; and an available Skype app, as well as the Kindle ereader (see Figure 1-1). In addition, the WPS Office productivity app is built in and allows you to work with word processor, spreadsheet, and presentation documents.

Just because a particular type of app doesn't come preinstalled on your Fire tablet doesn't mean you can't get one — you can, and often for free.

At this point, the selection of apps available for Android devices isn't nearly as robust as those available for Apple devices, but that is changing. See Chapter 14 for a list of ten or so apps that can flesh out your Fire tablet with popular features such as a budget tracker, games, weather reporter, and drawing app.

Preinstalled functionality

Here's a rundown of the functionality you get out of the box from prein-stalled apps:

- ✔ Ereader to read both books and periodicals
- ✔ Music player
- ✔ Video player
- ✔ Audiobook player
- ✔ Contacts app
- ✔ Calendar app
- ✔ Clock app
- ✔ Docs document reader for Word, PDF, RTF, and HTML format files
- ✔ Silk web browser

- Camera and Photos (see Figure 1-2) in which you can view and make edits (such as rotate, change brightness and adjust for red-eye, and crop) to photos
- Email client, to set up the Fire tablet to access your existing email accounts
- Integration for Goodreads, Facebook, and Twitter
- WPS Office for simple word processing, presentation, and spreadsheet functionality

ARCADIA FALLS: A NOVEL

over this conundrum until I made myself quite sick with worrying. Vera could not help but notice how preoccupied I was and it raised in her once more the old demon of jealousy. She began to resent the time I spent posing for Nash and would even remark upon it over dinner, asking Nash quite pointedly if he wasn't done yet, and hadn't he committed his subject to memory enough to be able to continue without a model.

"Every time I look at Lily, I see something I hadn't seen before," he answered.

Vera's face turned an angry red. Nothing infuriated her more than the idea that Nash knew me better than she did. The truth is that Nash *did* see me more clearly than Vera did. I'm afraid it was obvious to everyone that she was jealous of him, although I think that the girls mostly thought that she was jealous of his talent and success, not of *me*. Ivy wasn't so blind, though. She watched me carefully whenever Vera and Nash and I were in the same room, and she noted the growing hostility between Vera and Nash. I could see how uncomfortable it made her. She might be infatuated with Virgil Nash, but she still idolized Vera. She couldn't bear to see the two of them at odds. Finally last week I went to Nash and begged him to leave Arcadia. I said nothing about Ivy but spoke only of Vera's jealousy.

"As long as you are here, there will be no peace between us,"

Location 4694   73%

Figure 1-1: Where it all started, with Kindle ereader functionality.

Figure 1-2: Use the Photos app to view photos and edit them.

Check out the apps stored in the Cloud (meaning that these apps are stored at Amazon, rather than being preinstalled on your device) by tapping Apps on the Home screen and then tapping the Cloud tab. Here, you may find a number of free apps, such as a Wifi Analyzer (to check your Wi-Fi connection), free games, and more.

Here are some of the things you can use your Fire tablet for:

- ✔ Shopping at Amazon for music, video, apps, books, and periodicals, and viewing or playing that content, covered in Chapter 6.

- ✔ Storing Amazon-purchased content in the Amazon Cloud Drive and playing music and video selections from the Cloud instead of downloading them to your device. Amazon content doesn't count toward your

Amazon Cloud Drive storage limit (20GB), but other content backed up there does. Note that you can go to `www.amazon.com/clouddrive` and purchase anywhere from 20GB for $10 a year up to 1000GB of storage for $500.

✔ Sending documents to yourself at a Kindle email address that's assigned when you register your device (see Chapter 4 for more about setting up your Fire tablet, and Chapter 12 for more about using your Kindle email address to send documents to your Fire tablet).

✔ *Sideloading* (transferring) content from your computer to your Fire tablet by using a micro USB cable that comes with the tablet. Using this cable (see Figure 1-3), you can copy photos, music, videos, and documents (Word or PDF) from any computer onto your Fire tablet. See Chapters 6 and 8 for more about ways to get content onto your Fire.

✔ Making video calls using the free Skype for the Fire tablet app.

✔ "Flinging" movies from your device to your large-screen TV using the Second Screen feature.

Figure 1-3: The Fire's micro USB cable and a power adapter.

The magic of Whispersync

If you've ever owned a Kindle ereader, you know that downloading Amazon content to it has always been seamless. All you need for this process is access to a Wi-Fi or 4G network. Then you simply order a book, music, or a video, and within moments, it appears on your Kindle device.

The Fire tablet enjoys the same kind of easy download capability for books, audiobooks, music, video, and periodicals.

Whispersync helps sync items such as bookmarks you've placed in ebooks or the last place you watched in a video across various devices. For example, say you have the Kindle ereader app on your Fire tablet, PC, and smartphone. Wherever you left off reading, whatever notes you entered, and whatever pages you've bookmarked will be synced among all the devices without your having to lift a finger. (See Chapter 8 for details on notes, bookmarking, and more features of the ereader.)

Immersion Reading is a feature that uses Whispersync to allow you to play an audiobook and have the current word that's being spoken highlighted in the text. This feature supposedly aids in reader retention, so it might be a nice match for those late-night study sessions with textbooks.

Using content libraries

As I state earlier, the Fire tablet is meant to be a device you use to consume media, meaning that you can use it to play/read all kinds of music, movies, TV shows, podcasts, ebooks, audiobooks, magazines, and newspapers. Amazon has built up a huge amount of content, from print (see Figure 1-4) to audio books via its subsidiary Audible (more than 22 million) to movies, TV shows, songs, books, magazines, audiobooks, apps, and games. Count on these numbers to have risen by the time you read this: Amazon continues to rack up deals with media groups such as Fox Broadcasting and PBS to make even more content available on a regular basis.

Tap a library — such as Books, Music, or Videos — on the Fire tablet Home screen, and you can find various kinds of content in the AmazonStore — by tapping the Store button. Tap Newsstand to shop for periodicals (see Figure 1-5) and Music to shop for songs and albums; tap Video and you go directly to the Amazon Video Store. Tap Apps to shop the Amazon Appstore. If you download content, it's contained in one of these libraries, which have tabs to display content on the device, and you can read or play it even if you're not connected to the Internet. All the content you purchase is backed up on the Amazon Cloud Drive automatically.

Figure 1-4: The Kindle Bookstore offers more than 1 million books for the Kindle ereader app.

Another form of content that you get for free is the information contained in the IMDb, a database owned by Amazon. This information is used by the X-Ray feature to show you information about actors and characters in videos, song lyrics in music, and characters or other information referenced in books.

When you own a Fire tablet and have a Prime account, you can take advantage of the Kindle Owner's Lending Library, where you can choose from more than 200,000 books to borrow at no charge for as long as you like. If you have an Amazon Prime membership, you can also get one free book a month for your permanent library.

TIP

If you're concerned about kids who access content over a Fire tablet, check out the limitations you can place using the parental controls (see Chapter 5) or buy them their own Kids Edition of Fire for even more control over their content.

See Chapter 6 for more about buying content and apps for your Fire tablet.

Figure 1-5: Amazon's magazine selection is constantly growing.

Browsing with Amazon Silk

Silk is the Internet browser for Fire tablets (see Figure 1-6). Silk is simple to use, but the real benefits of Amazon Silk are all about browsing performance.

Figure 1-6: Amazon Silk offers simple-to-use browsing tools.

Amazon Silk is touted as a "Cloud-accelerated split browser." In plain English, this means that the browser can use the power of Amazon's servers to load the pages of a website quickly. Because parts of the process of loading web pages are handled not on your Fire tablet but on servers in the Cloud, your pages should display faster.

In addition, you get what's called a *persistent connection,* which means that your tablet is always connected to the Amazon Internet backbone (the routes that data travels to move among networks online) whenever it has access to a Wi-Fi connection.

Silk comes with a Reading View, which removes from your browser view all but the written content in certain online articles, which gets rid of distracting ads. In addition, you get easy-to-use navigation tools and content pages that let you view web content by categories, such as Most Visited and Bookmarks. See Chapter 7 for more about using the Silk browser and Reading View.

The Fire tablet 6- and 7-inch models can connect only via Wi-Fi; the 8.9-inch Fire tablet 4G LTE Wireless models have both Wi-Fi access and 4G LTE access, so they can connect to a cellular network just as your mobile phone does.

Another touted capability of Silk is the way it filters content to deliver it faster. Say you open a news site, such as MSN or CNN. Obviously, millions of others are accessing these pages on the same day. If most of those folks choose to open the Entertainment page after reading the home page of the site, Silk essentially predicts what page you might open next and preloads it. If you choose to go to that page, too, it appears instantly.

A world of color on the display

The display on Fire tablets offers a high-resolution screen that makes for very crisp colors when you're watching that hit movie or reading a colorful magazine (see Figure 1-7). The 8.9-inch model offers the highest resolution of the bunch.

In-plane switching is a technology that gives you a wide viewing angle on the Fire tablet screens. The result is that if you want to share your movie with a friend sitting next to you on the couch, she'll have no problem seeing what's on the screen from that side angle.

Figure 1-7: The bright display on Fire tablets makes media shine.

In addition, the screen is coated with layers of gorilla glass that make it extra strong, so it should withstand most of the bumps and scratches you throw at it.

Of course, you should avoid dropping your Fire tablet, exposing it to extreme temperatures, or spilling liquids on it. The User Guide also advises that if you do spill liquids, you shouldn't heat the device in your microwave to dry it off. (Perhaps a case of tablet maintenance advice for real dummies?)

Understanding the value of Amazon Prime

Fire tablets come with one free month of Amazon Prime. I've been an Amazon Prime member for years, so I'm a bit prejudiced about this: I can tell you firsthand that this service is one of the best deals out there. During your free month, Prime will allow you to get a lot of perks, such as free two-day shipping on thousands of items sold through Amazon, a free ebook, and free instant videos.

If you decide to pick up the service after your free month, it will cost you $99 a year. So, what do you get for your money?

Without sounding like an Amazon marketing person, I will tell you that Prime includes free two-day shipping on millions of items and overnight shipping for only a few dollars more. Not every item offered on Amazon is eligible for Prime, but enough are that it's a wonderful savings in time and money over the course of a year. You can probably pay for the membership with the free shipping on the first two or three orders you place. And, getting your Prime stuff in only two days every time is sweet.

In addition, Prime membership gives you access to Prime Instant Videos (see Figure 1-8), which gives you access to thousands of movies and TV shows that can be streamed to your Fire tablet absolutely free. I'm not talking obscure 1970s sleepers here: Recent additions to Prime Instant Videos include TV shows such as *Downton Abbey* and *Alpha House,* and award-winning movies such as *Star Trek: Into Darkness* and *Skyfall.*

If you have already paid for a yearly subscription to Amazon Prime, you don't get an extra month for free, sad to say. And if you don't have a Prime account, your 30 days of a free account starts from the time you activate your Fire tablet, not the first time you make a Prime purchase or stream a Prime Instant Video. So, my suggestion is to start using it right away to take full advantage and decide whether the paid membership is for you.

Figure 1-8: The Prime Instant Videos service adds new videos all the time; check it out!

2

Firing Up Your Fire Tablet

*T*he basics of using Fire tablet are . . . well, pretty basic. You start by turning it on and following a set of extremely short and simple instructions to set it up and register it, and then you can begin to get acquainted with its features.

In this chapter, I help you understand what comes in the box, explore the interface (what you see on the screen), and start to use your fingers to interact with the touchscreen. To round out your introduction, you get a sense of how things are organized on a Fire tablet Home screen and how to transfer data between your computer and tablet.

Get Going with Your Fire Tablet

There's always a logical place to start building a fire. In this case, forget the kindling and matches, and get started by examining what comes in the Fire tablet box and learn how to turn your new tablet on and off. The first time you turn on a Fire tablet, you register it and link it to your Amazon account so you can shop till you drop.

Also, although your device probably comes with a decent battery charge, at some point, you'll inevitably have to charge the battery, so I cover that in the section "Charging the battery."

Opening the box

When your Fire tablet arrives, it will come in a black box in a dark gray sleeve that sports the image of the Kindle Home screen (see Figure 2-1). The Fire tablet rests on top of a piece of cardboard, with a black card that contains some Fire tablet basics printed on both sides. Finally, beneath the Fire tablet is a slot containing a micro USB cable that you use to connect the device to a computer and charge the Fire tablet. That's it.

Remove the protective plastic from the device, and you're ready to get going.

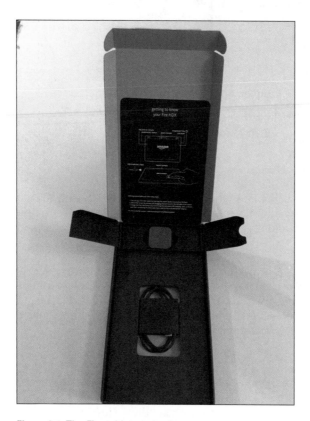

Figure 2-1: The Fire tablet packaging.

Turning your Fire tablet on and off

After you get the tablet out of its packaging, it's time to turn it on. The 8.9-inch Fire tablet sports a Power button on the back near the top when you hold it in portrait orientation (see Figure 2-2). On the back near the bottom is the volume rocker. On the top is a slot for charging the device; on the bottom is a headphone jack. On the 6- or 7-inch devices, the power, headphone jack, and slot for the cable to charge the devices is on the top of the device.

Figure 2-2: The Power button sits on the back top of your 8.9-inch Fire tablet.

To turn the device on, press the Power button. If you're starting up for the first time, you're taken through a series of setup screens (see "Setting up your Fire tablet," later in this chapter, for more about this). After you go through the setup process and register your Fire tablet, you see the Home screen shown in Figure 2-3.

The Status bar gives you information about items such as your device's battery charge, as well as your network connection and time. The list of libraries (Games, Apps, and so on) provides access to libraries of content and related Amazon Stores. In the middle of the screen is a carousel of your most recently used content and apps, and along the bottom is a grid of favorite apps (the Silk browser, Email, Help, Calendar, Contacts, and so on). You can find more about the elements on the Home screen in the section "Getting to Know the Interface," later in this chapter.

Figure 2-3: The Fire tablet Home screen.

If you want to lock your Fire tablet, which is akin to putting a laptop computer to sleep, press the Power button. To shut down your Kindle, from any screen (except the Lock screen) press and hold the Power button until a message appears offering you the options to Power Off or Cancel, as shown in Figure 2-4.

If your Fire tablet becomes nonresponsive, you can press and hold the Power button for 20 seconds. After the screen goes black, press the Power button again and it should come to life again.

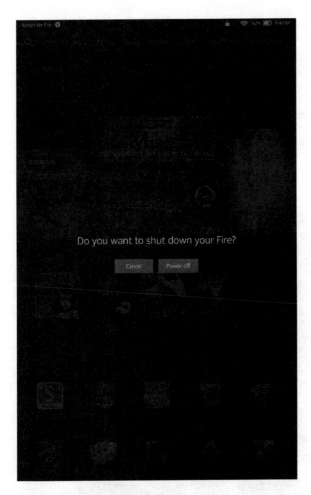

Figure 2-4: You can proceed to shut down your device, or cancel and return to the Home screen.

Getting to know the touchscreen

Before you work through the setup screens for your Fire tablet, it will help if you to get to know the basics of navigating the touchscreen — especially if you've never used a touchscreen before:

- ✔ Swipe down from the Status bar at the top of the Home screen to display Quick Settings (most commonly used settings covered in Chapter 3) and Notifications (such as download status, alarms, and email messages in your Inbox); swipe up to hide the Quick Settings and Notifications.

- ✔ Tap an item to select it or open it.

✔ Tap the Home button (shaped like a little house) at any time to return to the Home screen.

✔ If your Fire tablet goes dark after a period of inactivity, tap the Power button and then swipe the Unlock button on the Lock screen (see Figure 2-5) from right to left to go to the Home screen.

✔ Double-tap the screen to enlarge text, and double-tap again to return the text to its original size. *Note:* This works only in certain locations, such as when displaying a web page in the Silk browser. Double-tapping in some other locations, such as when reading a book or viewing a video, will display tools you can use to perform certain actions.

Figure 2-5: Swipe the Unlock button to go to the Home screen.

✔ Place your fingers on the screen and spread them apart to zoom in (enlarge the view); then pinch them together to zoom out on the current view (reduce the view). This action only works in selected apps, such as the Silk browser.

✔ Swipe left or tap the left edge of a page to move to the next page in the ereader. Swipe to the right or tap the right edge of a page to move to the previous page in a book.

✔ In many apps, tap the three horizontal lines in the upper-left corner to display the Navigation panel, offering options for working in the app.

✔ Swipe up and down to scroll up and down a web page.

These touchscreen gestures will help you get around most of the content and setup screens you encounter in the Fire tablet.

If you prefer to use your Fire tablet and its touchscreen without holding the device in your hands, consider getting the new Origami cover, which you can use as a stand for your Fire tablet. Ranging from $50 to $65, depending on whether you opt for leather or a less expensive material, this clever cover not only protects your Fire tablet but also acts as a useful stand to hold it upright while you work with it.

Setting up your Fire tablet

When you turn the Fire tablet on for the first time, you see a series of screens that help you set up and register the device. Don't worry: There aren't many questions, and you know all the answers.

At some point during this setup procedure, you may be prompted to plug your adapter in, if your battery charge is low. You may also be notified that the latest Fire operating system is downloading and that you have to wait for that process to complete before you can move forward.

In most cases Amazon will have pre-registered your Amazon account to the device so you shouldn't have to register it yourself. However, if you don't have an Amazon account, you'll get a chance to create one during setup. During the setup procedure you'll also make choices about your language and country, time zone, and the Wi-Fi connection you'll use to go online.

After you work your way through the setup prompts, you see a Welcome screen. Tap Get Started to see the first of several screens that help you learn to navigate the Fire tablet by swiping left, up, and down on its screen. At the end of the series, on the screen titled Congratulations, tap Finish to go to the Fire tablet Home screen shown in Figure 2-6.

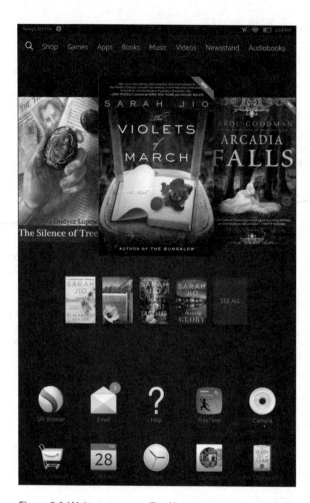

Figure 2-6: Welcome to your Fire Home screen.

When you register your Fire tablet to your Amazon account, a Kindle email address is created. You can use this email address to send or have other people send documents to you, which then appear in your Docs library on your Fire tablet, or photos, which appear in your Photos app. See Chapter 12 for more about working with Docs.

Charging the battery

According to Amazon, the 8.9-inch tablet has a battery life of about 12 hours for Wi-Fi–connected activities such as web browsing, streaming movies, and listening to music from the Cloud. The smaller tablets support about 8 hours of so-called "mixed-use" battery life. If you're a bookworm who's more into the printed word than media, you'll be happy to hear that Amazon claims you get up to about 17 hours of reading downloaded books with Wi-Fi turned off.

Whichever model Fire you have, you'll need to charge it now and then. You charge the battery by using the provided micro USB cable and power adapter. Attach the smaller end of the micro USB cable to your Fire tablet's micro USB port, located along the top of the device when held in portrait orientation (refer to Figure 2-2), and the other end of the micro USB cable into the power adapter, which you then plug into a wall outlet. If the tablet is completely out of juice, it will take about four to six hours to charge it; otherwise, an hour or so is usually sufficient.

A battery indicator on the Status bar runs across the top of the screen; you can check this to see if your battery is running low. The more white there is in the battery icon, the more battery time you have left. A notification appears and the left side of the icon turns red when the battery is very low. If you also want to see a text percentage next to the battery, go to Settings⇨ Device Options and turn the Show Battery Percentage in Status Bar On/Off switch to On.

Getting to Know the Interface

The interface you see on the Kindle Home screen (see Figure 2-7) is made up of four items. At the top is the Status bar, which includes icons that tell you

- ✓ The name of your Fire tablet
- ✓ The number of current notifications
- ✓ Whether you're in Airplane mode or connected to a network
- ✓ Remaining battery life

The Status bar icons are explained in more detail later in this chapter.

Below the Status bar is a set of buttons that take you to the Fire tablet libraries that contain various types of content such as Books, Videos, Games, Apps, and Audiobooks. This row also contains a button to Shop at the Amazon Store, open the Silk browser by tapping Web, view Photos or Docs, and look at special offers if your Fire tablet doesn't have ads disabled. You can swipe left or right on this row of buttons to display more.

In the middle of the screen is the Carousel (refer to Figure 2-7). The Carousel contains images of items you recently used. You can flick with your finger to scroll through these items, and tap any item to open it. The item on the far left is the most recently viewed, and others are shown in the order in which you last used them. You can scroll through these items, which places another item at the top of the Carousel stack. This effect is easiest to see in portrait orientation; Amazon's recommendations for similar content are displayed in thumbnails underneath the active item (except for Docs).

Figure 2-7: This graphical interface is fun to move around with the flick of a finger.

Accessing Fire tablet libraries

Fire tablet libraries are where you access downloaded content, as well as content stored by Amazon in the Cloud. Libraries (with the exception of the Docs and Photos libraries) also offer shopping options when you display the Left Nav menu, which you can tap to go online to browse and buy more content.

Understanding the Cloud and your Fire tablet

Everything you buy using Fire tablet features is purchased through Amazon or its affiliates on the Amazon site. That content is downloaded to your device through a Wi-Fi connection, unless you have a Fire 4G LTE Wireless model.

When you purchase content, you can choose whether to keep it in the Amazon Cloud or download it to your Fire tablet. If you download it, you can access it whether or not you're in range of a Wi-Fi network. At any time, you can remove content from the device, and it will be archived in the Cloud for you to stream to your device (music or video) or re-download (music, video, books, and magazines) anytime you like as long as you have a Wi-Fi connection. Keeping content you're not currently using in the Amazon Cloud can save space on your device.

Tap any library button to open a library of downloaded and archived content: Games, Apps, Books, Music, Videos, Newsstand, or Audiobooks. When you tap all of these (except Videos), your library of content is displayed along with a Store button to take you to the associated Amazon Store. The Videos button works a bit differently in that it opens to the Amazon Store rather than a library. You can tap the Left Nav button and then tap Your Video Library to go to your library. This difference is due to the fact that, in most cases, it's not very prudent to download a lot of video content to your Fire tablet because this type of content takes up so much of your device's memory. It's preferable to play video from Amazon's Cloud (a process called *streaming*).

There's also a Web button among the list of libraries that you can tap to open the Silk web browser. Find out more about going online and using the browser in Chapter 7.

In a library, such as many of the screens in the Music library shown in Figure 2-8, you can tap the Device or Cloud tab located at the top of the screen. The Device tab shows you only content you have downloaded; the Cloud tab displays all your purchases or free content stored in Amazon's Cloud library, including content you've downloaded to the Fire tablet.

You can download archived content to your device at any time or remove downloaded content from your device, and it's still stored in the Cloud. You can also view the contents of libraries in different ways, depending on which library you're in. For example, you can view the Music library contents by categories such as Songs, Artists, and Albums.

See Chapter 6 for more about buying content, Chapter 8 for information about reading books and magazines, and Chapters 9 and 10, respectively, for more about playing music and video.

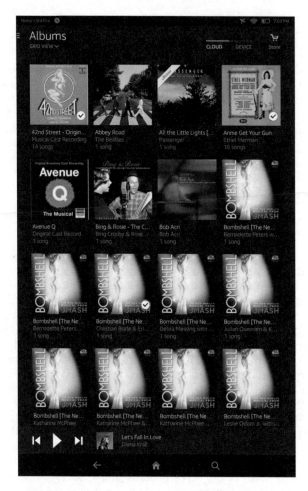

Figure 2-8: Your Music library provides access to all your musical content.

It's possible to download video, which is useful if you'll be out of range of a Wi-Fi connection, but I recommend that you remove the content from your device when you're done watching and back in Wi-Fi range. Removing a movie from your Fire tablet involves locating it in the library, pressing it with your finger, and choosing Delete Download from the menu that appears. For a TV show, press and hold the item and then choose View Season Details from the menu that appears. Tap the episode and on the details that appear, tap Download Options. In the dialog that appears, tap Delete Downloads.

As mentioned before, you can also sideload content you've obtained from other sources, such as iTunes, to your Fire tablet libraries. *Sideloading* involves connecting the micro USB cable that came with your Fire tablet to your computer (with the power adapter removed) and then copying content to the tablet. See the section "Using a Micro USB Cable to Transfer Data," later in this chapter, for more about this process.

Playing with the Carousel

Many of us have fond memories of riding a carousel at the fair as kids. The Fire tablet Carousel may not bring the same thrill, but it does have its charms as you swipe through it to see a revolving display of recently used books, audiobooks, music, videos, websites, docs, and apps (see Figure 2-9).

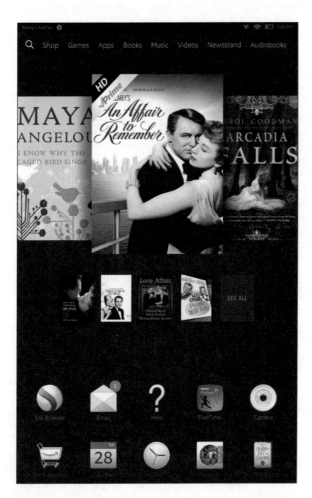

Figure 2-9: The Fire tablet's Carousel makes recently used content available.

If you've used an Android smartphone, you may have encountered the Carousel concept. On a Fire tablet, items you've used recently are displayed here chronologically, with the item you used most recently on top. You can swipe your finger to the right or left to flick through the Carousel contents. When you find an item you want to view or play, tap to open it.

Whatever you tap opens in the associated player or reader. Music will open in the Amazon MP3 music player; video in the Amazon Video player; and docs, books, and magazines in the Kindle ereader.

In addition to using the Carousel to view content and apps, you can use Quickswitch, a feature that allows you to swipe from the Options bar on any screen other than the Home screen to see a scrollable list of recently played content and recently used apps. Scroll to the right or left to find an item and tap it to open it.

Getting on the grid

When you're on a roll using your Fire tablet to access all kinds of content, the Carousel, which contains recently viewed content or apps, can get a bit crowded. You may have to swipe five or six times to find what you need. That's where Favorites comes in.

The concept of Favorites is probably familiar to you from working with web browsers, in which Favorites is a feature that allows you to put websites you visit frequently in a Favorites folder. On the Fire tablet, Favorites is also a place for saving frequently used content and apps; Favorites takes the form of a grid of thumbnails at the bottom of the Home screen.

If, for example, you're reading a book you open often or you play a certain piece of music frequently, place it in the Favorites area of the Fire tablet, and you can find it more quickly.

By default, Favorites includes commonly used apps, including:

- FreeTime Unlimited
- Camera
- Shop Amazon
- Clock
- Calendar
- Contacts
- Settings

Games and apps are automatically added to Favorites when you download them. To pin an item such as music or a book to Favorites, tap Apps at the top of the screen, then press and hold an app and tap the Add button. From the menu that appears, tap To Home (see Figure 2-10).

Figure 2-10: Pin items to your Home screen by using this menu.

To remove content from Favorites, press and hold an item in the grid. The Remove button appears. You can tap additional items if you like and then tap Remove (see Figure 2-11). Though deleted from the Favorites grid, the item is still available to you on the Carousel and in the related library.

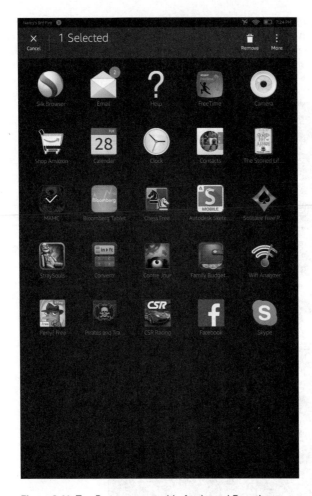

Figure 2-11: Tap Remove to get rid of selected Favorites.

Getting clues from the Status bar

The Status bar runs across the top of every Fire tablet screen, just like the Status bar on your mobile phone. This bar, shown in Figure 2-12, provides information about your device name, notifications, your network connection, your battery charge, and the time.

Search   Time

Device name   Battery charge

Notifications   Wi-Fi signal strength

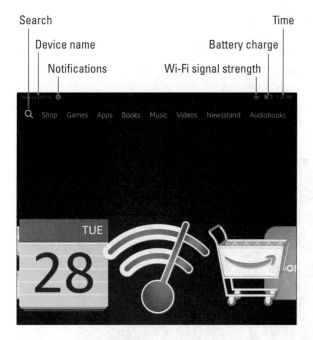

Figure 2-12: The various tools and settings available on the Status bar.

Here's a rundown of what you'll find on the Status bar:

- ✒ **Device name:** First is the name of your Fire tablet, such as Nancy's Kindle or Nancy's 2nd Kindle.

- ✒ **Notifications:** A number sometimes appears just to the right of the device name, such as 2, to indicate that you have that many Notifications. Notifications can come from the Fire tablet system announcing a completed download, or the email client announcing that a new email has arrived in one of your account inboxes, for example. To view all your notifications, swipe down from the Status bar, and a list appears (see Figure 2-13).

- ✒ **Airplane Mode/Bluetooth:** These icons appear on the right side of the Status bar when either Airplane mode or Bluetooth is turned on. The Bluetooth icon displays in a blue color when another Bluetooth device is connected.

✔ **Wireless:** When Airplane mode is off, that icon is replaced by an icon showing your Wi-Fi connection status. If the icon is lit up, you're connected. The more bright white bars in the symbol, the stronger the connection.

✔ **Battery charge:** The battery icon to the right side of the Status bar indicates the percentage of charge remaining on your battery.

✔ **Current time:** The item at the far right of the Status bar is the current time, based on the time zone you specified when setting up the Fire tablet.

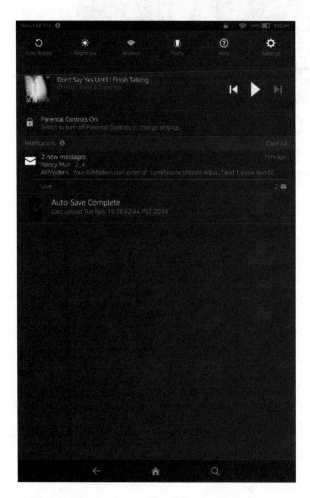

Figure 2-13: The list of current notifications that you can display from any screen.

You can swipe down from the top of the screen to access Quick Settings. Quick Settings offer the most commonly used settings. Use these items to turn the Auto-Rotate feature on or off (if it's on, when you turn your Fire tablet the screen moves around in sync with its orientation), adjust screen brightness, set up your Wi-Fi connection, turn Quiet Time on or off in the smaller tablets, and turn on the Firefly feature in the largest Fire tablet. Tap the Mayday button on the 8.9-inch Fire tablets to contact an Amazon tech advisor; tap the Help button to access Help options, including the live Mayday support feature if you own an 8.9-inch Fire tablet. To access the full Fire tablet Settings menu, tap Settings on the right of the Quick Settings bar. See Chapter 3 for a detailed breakdown of all Fire tablet settings.

To use Mayday, just tap the Help button and, on a Fire 8.9-inch tablet, tap Connect. In a few seconds (about 15 or so, depending on how busy the Mayday folks are), a small window appears in the bottom-right corner with the image of your tech advisor in it. Start asking questions and let the advisor explain, circle items on your screen, or even take over your device and perform procedures for you.

The often-present, ever-changing Options bar

The Options bar runs along the bottom or right side of your Fire tablet screen, depending on which app or library you open and how the device is oriented. In some apps, the Options bar is always visible; if the Options bar is hidden, you will typically (but not always) see a small black tab with lines on it, either on the right side or at the bottom of the screen, which you can swipe to display the Options bar. In other cases (as in the ereader app), just tap the screen and the Options bar appears.

The items offered on the Options bar change, depending on what library or app you're using, but they always include a Home button, Search button, and back arrow to move back one screen. In addition, you'll sometimes see a Menu button when you tap the Options bar. This icon, which looks like a little box with three lines in it, makes available commonly used settings for the currently displayed feature, such as a button to switch to list view rather than thumbnails. Figure 2-14 shows you the options available on the Apps library screen. From left to right in the figure, these buttons are Back, the Home button, and Search.

Use the Home button to jump back to the Fire tablet Home screen from anywhere. On some screens where it would be annoying to be distracted by the Options bar, such as the ereader, you may have to tap the screen to make the Options bar appear.

Figure 2-14: The Options bar offers different options based on which app is displayed.

The Navigation panel

When you tap the Left Nav button in the top-left corner of most apps, the Navigation panel appears. You access this panel by tapping the Left Nav button (represented by three horizontal lines).

The Navigation panel, shown in Figure 2-15, contains different options based on what app or content you're working with. For example, in a book, the Navigation panel displays a list of articles; in the Silk browser, it provides shortcuts labeled Bookmarks, Most Visited Sites, Downloads, and more.

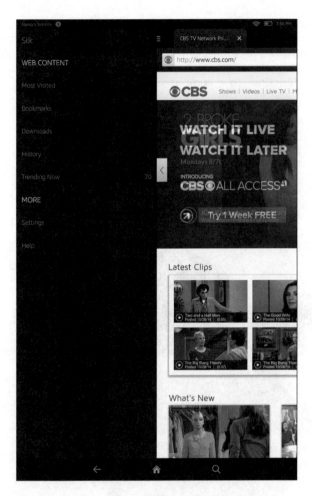

Figure 2-15: Choices here change based on what app or content you're viewing.

Using a Micro USB Cable to Transfer Data

It's easy to purchase or rent content from Amazon, which you can choose to download directly to your Fire tablet or stream from the Amazon Cloud. However, you may want to get content from other places, such as iTunes or your Pictures folder on your computer, and play or view it on your Fire tablet.

To transfer content to your Fire tablet, you use the micro USB cable that came with your tablet. This cable has a USB connector on one end that you can plug into your PC or Mac, and a micro USB connector on the other that fits into the micro USB port on your Fire tablet (which is located on the top near the Power button when holding a Fire tablet in portrait orientation; refer to Figure 2-2).

Attach the micro USB end (see Figure 2-16) to your Fire tablet and the USB end to your computer. Your Fire tablet should then appear as a drive in File Explorer in Windows 8 or later (see Figure 2-17) or the Mac Finder. You can now click and drag files from your hard drive to the Fire tablet or use the copy and paste functions to accomplish the same thing.

Figure 2-16: The micro USB cable.

Using this process, you can transfer apps, photos, docs, music, ebooks, audiobooks, and videos from your computer to your Fire tablet. Then, just tap the relevant library (such as Books for ebooks and Music for songs) to read or play the content on your Fire tablet.

If you want to transfer content from your Fire tablet to your computer, you have two options: Share the content via email, or access the content through the Amazon Cloud Drive using your computer's browser.

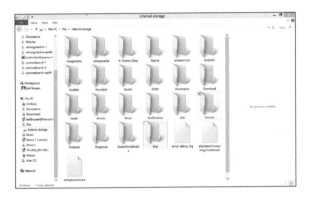

Figure 2-17: Fire tablet contents shown as a drive in File Explorer.

 You can also upload content to your Amazon Cloud Drive using your computer, and that content will then be available on your Fire tablet. Go to Amazon.com, search for Cloud Drive Installer, download the app, and then use the app to access your Cloud Drive on your computer and manage the drive's contents.

 You can share photos via Email, Facebook, or Twitter. Tap Photos on the Home screen, locate a photo, and press and hold it. On the menu that appears at the top right of the screen, tap Share and then choose the method of sharing. Fill out the email, Facebook, or Twitter form that appears and tap Send or Post. Using this method, you can share with yourself or others. You will find Share features in several apps; for example, in the Silk browser, tap the menu on the Options bar and tap Share Page to share the current page's URL.

3

Exploring Fire Tablet Quick Settings

*W*hen you first take your Fire tablet out of the box, Amazon has provided you with default settings that will work for most people most of the time. However, we've all gotten used to being able to personalize our experience with phone and computer devices, so you may be curious about the various ways in which you can make your Fire tablet work uniquely for you.

A tablet device such as Fire has dozens of settings that help you manage your tablet experience. Some of these settings are discussed in the chapters that cover individual apps, such as the Amazon video player (Chapter 10) and Contacts (Chapter 11). But you may need to review other settings when you start using your Fire tablet. In this chapter I cover Fire's Quick Settings, the first tier of settings that appear when you swipe down from the top of the screen. Quick Settings are some of the more commonly used settings on Fire tablets.

Opening Quick Settings

In this fast-paced day and age, quick is the name of the game for most of us, so Amazon has provided you with Quick Settings to streamline your settings experience.

You access both a short list of commonly used settings (Quick Settings) and all the more detailed settings for your Fire tablet by swiping downward from the top of the screen.

Figure 3-1 shows the settings that you can control from the Quick Settings menu, each of which is described in the following sections.

Figure 3-1: Quick Settings control the settings that you access most often.

Controlling spin with Auto-Rotate

When you turn your Fire tablet around, the screen automatically rotates from a portrait orientation to a landscape orientation (unless you're using an app that doesn't support rotation), depending on how you're holding it at the moment. This is great if you decide you want to slip to a different orientation in some apps to see your content more easily. However, if you don't want the orientation to keep flipping whenever you move the device, you can turn off the Auto-Rotate feature. This is handy, for example, when you're lying on the beach reading a book and don't want it to flip to another orientation every time you turn to even out your suntan.

To toggle this feature on or off, tap this setting in Quick Settings to toggle between Auto-Rotate, which lets you freely rotate as you move the Fire into different orientations, and Rotation Locked, which locks the screen in its current orientation.

Turning up the Brightness

By turning up the screen brightness on your Fire tablet, you may be able to see items more clearly. However, you should be aware that a higher brightness setting can eat up your battery power more quickly.

You can tap the Brightness setting in Quick Settings to display the Automatic Brightness On/Off switch (on the 8.9-inch Fire only) to turn on or off a feature that controls the brightness of the screen based on ambient light. You can also use the slider above this setting on any Fire model (see Figure 3-2) to adjust the brightness manually.

Working with Wireless settings

Tap the Wireless Quick Setting to access settings to control networks and Bluetooth connections (such as those to a Bluetooth mouse or keyboard). In addition, you'll see the Off/On switch for Airplane mode.

Airplane mode is a setting you should use if you're flying on a plane which makes quick access to it handy. With this setting off, your device won't search for available networks, which could conflict with airplane communications.

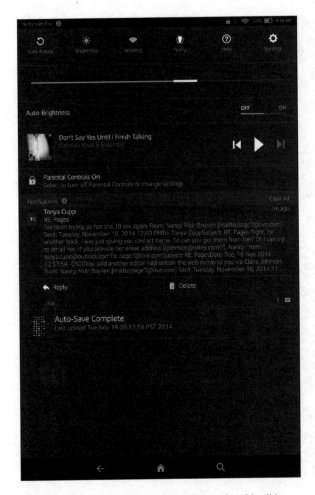

Figure 3-2: Adjust brightness manually by using this slider.

To toggle Airplane mode on and off, in Quick Settings, tap Wireless to display the Airplane mode On/Off button (see Figure 3-3). With Airplane mode set to On, no available networks appear.

To connect to a network from the Wireless settings, do this:

1. **Tap Wi-Fi and tap the On button.**

   A list of available networks appears.

2. **Tap an available network to join it.**

   Note that you may be asked to enter a password to access some networks. For more on Wireless and VPN settings, see Chapter 4.

Figure 3-3: Choose from the list of available networks.

Relaxing with Quiet Time

We all have times when we need to concentrate or relax, and at times like these, those little beeps and rings that come with notifications on your Fire can be, frankly, annoying.

Toggle the Quiet Time setting on and off, depending on whether you want to hear notification sounds and view notification pop-ups or not. When this setting is off, all those annoying sounds go away.

Note that Quick Settings only includes the Quiet Time setting in the 6- and 7-inch versions of the tablet.

Activating Firefly

The Quick Settings on 8.9-inch tablets contain a setting for Firefly. This new feature allows your tablet to identify text, such as movie posters or a CD cover, and display information about a movie, song, or other content.

When you tap the Firefly app, your front-facing camera turns on and little lights all over the screen try to identify whatever you're pointing at (see Figure 3-4). When your Fire recognizes any of over 240,000 movie titles, songs, or TV shows, it displays links to buy the content from the Amazon Store (see Figure 3-5).

Figure 3-4: Cute little lights appear while Fire tries to identify content.

Figure 3-5: Use these links to buy the content Firefly spotted.

Getting Help

The hottest help feature in your Fire tablet is Mayday, which provides a live support person who can walk you through a solution to your problem, take control of your screen and make changes or settings for you, or draw on your screen to show you what to do. Mayday is only available for the 8.9-inch tablet; those devices include a Mayday option when you tap Help in Quick Settings.

The technical advisor can't see you, though you can see him or her in a small window on your screen (see Figure 3-6).

You can pause the Mayday transmission if you need to type in a password so the support person can't see your screen when you do (or mute sound so you can talk with a friend). Both you and the support person have the ability to drag the small window containing his or her image around your screen so that you can see whatever you need to work with on the screen.

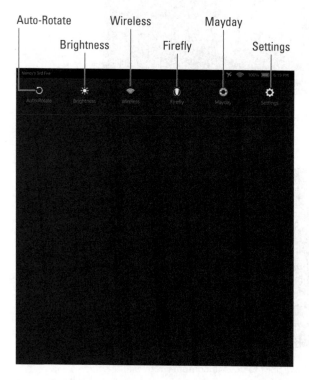

Figure 3-6: Help is a tap away with Mayday.

Mayday is available 7 days a week, 365 days of the year. Tap the Help button in Quick Settings (see Figure 3-7) and then tap the Connect button that appears to connect to a Mayday associate. It usually takes about 15 seconds for somebody to appear. If that person can't answer your question, he or she may put you on hold while checking with somebody else for an answer or testing the feature. In one case the person actually contacted somebody on Amazon's app team to figure out a solution.

Currently there is no time limit to how long you can stay on a Mayday call nor how many calls you can make. However, it remains to be seen whether Amazon can keep up with that level of support, and how many people might abuse the system to bend somebody's ear or test Amazon's patience.

If you have a smaller Fire tablet, what you'll see in Quick Settings is Help instead of Mayday. When you tap Help, you get four options:

- **Wireless** takes you to Wireless settings to troubleshoot a wireless connection.

- **User Guide** opens the Fire User Guide for text guidance to using the tablet.

- **Phone & Email** lets you tap Customer Service to connect via email or phone, or provide feedback to Amazon. Note that if you select Phone you see a form where you can enter your phone number so that Amazon can call you.

- **Tutorials** gives you access to the tutorials that you were offered when you first set up your Fire tablet. You can access them by tapping Tutorials and then choosing between Home Carousel, Favorites & Quick Settings, and Library Cloud/Device Toggle.

Figure 3-7: Tap this button to get help in seconds.

Finding Other Settings

Beyond what I discuss in the preceding section, there's one more item on the Quick Settings menu — Settings. Figure 3-8 shows you the many settings that appear when you tap the Settings button.

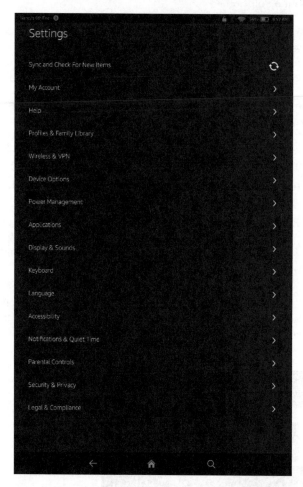

Figure 3-8: Plenty more settings are revealed when you tap Settings.

You won't need to change many of these settings very often because the way Fire works out of the box is usually very intuitive. But if you do find that you want to make an adjustment to settings such as the date and time, security, or parental controls, it's useful to know what's available.

Chapter 4 covers some of the options that you use while you're setting up network connections, power management, your Amazon account, and more. Other settings are covered in the associated chapter, such as sound settings in Chapter 9, "Playing Music," and email settings in Chapter 7, "Going Online."

4

Setting Up Your Fire

*W*hen you first take your Fire tablet out of the box, you might want to set it up so that some basics — modifying the accounts associated with your tablet, connecting to networks, and managing the sound and display — work the way you want them to.

Several settings are discussed in the chapters that cover individual apps, such as the Amazon video player (Chapter 10) and Contacts (Chapter 11). But as you get started with the Fire tablet, you should check out the basic settings covered in this chapter.

Understanding Accounts

The primary account you need to use your Fire tablet optimally is an Amazon account. This account is associated with a credit card, which makes shopping in various Amazon stores simple to do.

In addition, you can connect with your Facebook, Twitter, or Goodreads account. This allows you to use some features of Fire, such as importing Facebook contacts or posting content like photos to your social networking accounts. With Goodreads, you can share postings on books to friends who also have a Goodreads account.

Finally, you can set up an existing email account(s), such as one at Gmail or Outlook, to work through the Email app on your Fire tablet.

Working with My Account

Fire does much of what it does by accessing your Amazon account. You need to have an Amazon account to shop, access the Amazon Cloud Drive library online, and register your Fire tablet, for example.

The My Account option in Settings provides information about the account to which the device is registered (see Figure 4-1).

You can also view your Kindle email address on this screen. This address is useful because you can email documents to it, and those documents are then available on your Fire tablet.

If you sell or give your Fire tablet to somebody else (for example, if you bought it as a gift for somebody else), you can deregister to stop that person from accessing your account.

To remove this account from your Fire tablet, do this:

1. **From the My Account screen, tap the Deregister button.**

2. **Tap Deregister on the confirming window.**

   Because the obvious thing to do next is register your Fire tablet to another account (because so much depends on your having an associated account), you are presented with a Register button.

3. **The new owner should tap Register and fill in his or her Amazon username and password to register the device.**

If you deregister your account, don't register your Fire tablet, and leave this screen, you're placed in the introductory demo that appeared when you first set up your Fire tablet. When you finish that demo and tap any category, such as Books, you're again prompted to register your device to your Amazon account.

Once you've associated your tablet with an Amazon account, you can tap Amazon Account Settings (on the screen shown in Figure 4-1) to change settings for country, Amazon Prime, Payment Options, Subscriptions, and Personal Documents (documents you can send to your Kindle email address, which is provided when you register your tablet).

Managing social networks

The My Account screen also offers the option of managing social networking accounts.

Tap the Social Networks link to set up your Goodreads, Twitter, or Facebook account so that you can take advantage of built-in features for sharing information via these services.

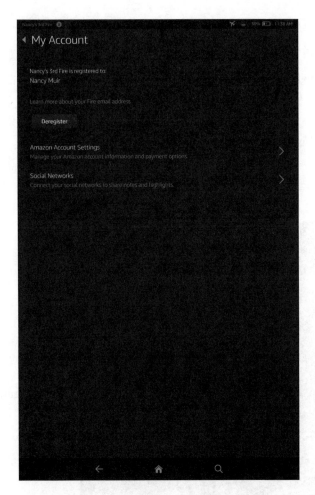

Figure 4-1: Check which Amazon account your device is registered to.

Setting up an email account

The Email app on your Fire tablet is what's referred to as an *email client,* which means that it doesn't provide an email account but provides the means of connecting with an email account or accounts allowing to work with them from the Email app.

Setting up your email on a Fire tablet involves providing information about one or more email accounts that you've already established with a provider such as Gmail.

Follow these steps to set up an email account the first time you use the app:

1. **Tap Email in the Favorites Grid.**

   The Mail app appears.

2. **From the Inbox, tap the Left Nav button.**

   The Left Nav panel appears.

3. **Tap Settings.**

4. **Tap Add Account.**

   The dialog box shown in Figure 4-2 appears.

Figure 4-2: Enter information about your email account.

5. **Enter your email address and then tap Next.**

6. **Enter your password and then tap Next.**

   Fire verifies your account and displays a Setup Complete screen.

7. **Choose to go to the email Inbox or add another account.**

   You can set up as many email accounts as you like. When you open the Email app, you see a Unified Inbox that combines messages from all accounts you set up, as well as individual Inboxes for each account.

Setting Up Wireless and Networks

Wireless is a pretty essential setting for using a Fire tablet. Without a Wi-Fi connection, you can't stream video or music, browse the Internet, shop at the various Amazon Stores, or send and receive email.

To work with wireless settings, first swipe down from the top of any screen and tap Wireless in the Quick Settings. The settings shown in Figure 4-3 appear.

Here's what each of these settings does:

- **Airplane Mode:** Turn this setting on or off. With Airplane mode on, you can't join a network.

- **Wi-Fi:** Tap Wi-Fi to go to more settings where you can turn the feature on or off. Note that turning Wi-Fi off may save some of your Fire tablet's battery life. With Wi-Fi on, you can tap a network on the list of available networks that appears to connect to it.

- **Bluetooth:** Tap here to access Bluetooth settings that allow you to enable and connect to a Bluetooth device such as a Bluetooth printer or cellphone.

- **VPN:** Use this setting to connect to a virtual private network (essentially a private network such as the one at your company).

- **Location-Based Services:** Tap to go to the setting to turn this feature on or off, depending on whether you want apps, such as Maps or Weather, to know your physical location.

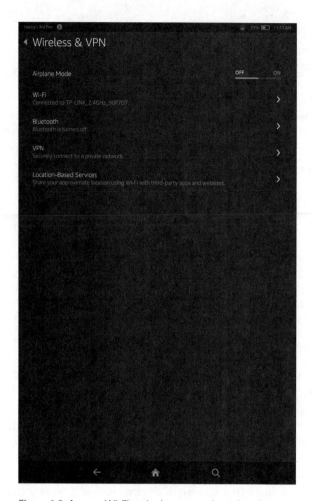

Figure 4-3: Access Wi-Fi and other network settings here.

Choosing Settings for Notifications and Quiet Time

Swipe down from the top of any screen and tap Settings, and then tap Notifications & Quiet Time. Here's what these two settings (shown in Figure 4-4) control.

Note that a shortcut for turning Quiet Time on and off is located in Quick Settings for the 6-inch and 7-inch models of Fire. That setting is replaced by Firefly in the 8.9-inch Fire.

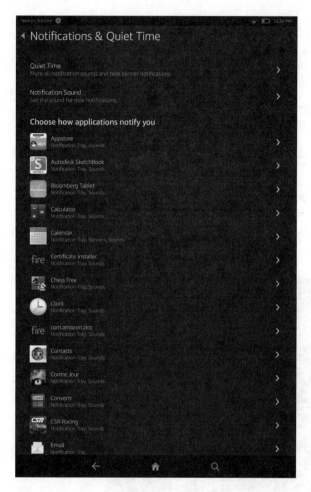

Figure 4-4: Notifications and Quiet Time are lumped together here.

The Notifications setting is all about how your Fire tablet lets you know about an event, such as a completed download or incoming message. Notifications may come from the arrival of a new email or a completed download, or an app might notify you of something (such as an appointment reminder from a calendar app that you may have downloaded). Notifications can be shown in the notification tray that appears when you swipe down from the top of the screen, or they can display a banner or play a sound.

Figure 4-4 shows a list apps that you can tap to select how you're notified about events related to them. For example, tap Clock and you can choose to show alarms in the notification tray; to show a banner style notification, or to play a notification sound.

Quiet Time turns off any notifications when you're performing certain types of actions or during a scheduled time. You can turn on Quiet Time and it stays in effect until you turn it off.

You can use the Quiet Time settings shown in Figure 4-5 to turn Quiet Time on or off, or set up a schedule of quiet times — for example, every day when it's time for your baby's nap or your yoga retreat. Tap the Quiet Time button to turn off audible alerts, and tap it again to turn them on. You can also set up a schedule for Quiet Time to activate, or tap one of the four preset check boxes to turn it on when you're performing specific activities, such as watching a movie or TV or listening to audiobooks.

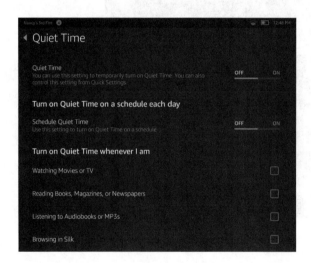

Figure 4-5: Quiet Time is a great way to get some time off from interruptions.

To set up a scheduled Quiet Time, follow these steps from the Notifications & Quiet Time settings:

1. **Tap the Schedule Quiet Time button to turn this feature on.**

2. **Use the From and To scroll bars to select start and end times for your Quiet Time.**

3. **Tap the Set Time button.**

Controlling Display and Sounds

With a tablet that's so media-centric, accessing music and video, as well as games that you can play with their accompanying screeches and sounds, it's important that you know how to control the volume.

If you tap Display & Sounds in Settings (see Figure 4-6), you can use a volume slider to increase or decrease the volume, as well as a slider you can adjust to dim or enhance the screen's brightness (dimmer to the left, brighter to the right). If you have an 8.9-inch Fire tablet, you also get an Auto-Brightness setting you can turn on to have Fire automatically adjust screen brightness depending on ambient light.

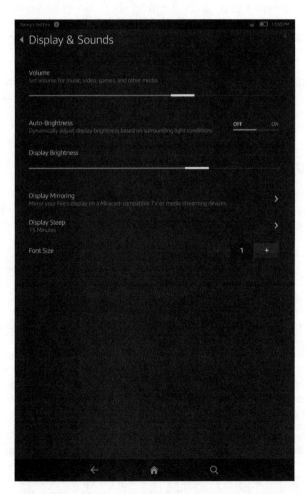

Figure 4-6: Display & Sounds settings are pretty darn simple to use.

Display & Sounds also allows you to manage your device's display, adjusting both Display Mirroring and Display Sleep. Here's what these settings control:

- **Display Mirroring (only available on the 8.9-inch Fire):** If you want to have your Fire tablet screen appear on your TV or a monitor, tap this setting to select a device that you can make discoverable (much as you make a cellphone discoverable to your car's Bluetooth setup). This setting is great for playing games on your Fire while also viewing the game on the larger screen.

- **Display Sleep:** After a certain period of inactivity, the Fire tablet screen will lock and go black to save battery power. You can adjust the length of this interval by tapping the arrow in this field and choosing from a list of time intervals that ranges from 30 seconds to one hour. You can also choose the option Never if you want your screen to be always on. However, remember that using the Never option will wear down your battery more quickly.

Finally, you can control the size of fonts that appear onscreen (such as library names or Settings) by tapping the + or – symbols on either side of the Font Size field.

New and Improved Accessibility Features

If you have challenges with manual dexterity (for example, carpal tunnel syndrome or arthritis), vision, or hearing, you may find that Accessibility features can help you in using your Fire tablet.

With Settings open, tap Accessibility.

Here's a quick rundown of available accessibility features:

- **Screen Reader:** Screen Reader audibly describes the actions you're taking on your Fire tablet. If you turn this setting on, the Reading Speed and Explore by Touch settings become available. Turning Screen Reader on also turns on Explore by Touch. The way you interact with your Fire changes dramatically when you turn these features on, so I strongly suggest you walk through the tutorial that's offered before you start to work with them. The most important thing to know is that when they are turned on, you have to tap and then double-tap items onscreen to perform an action.

- **Screen Magnifier:** Toggles on and off a feature that enlarges your entire screen. Once turned on, triple-tapping magnifies the screen, and you can then control the screen magnification by pinching your fingers inward or outward. Also, with Screen Magnifier on and the page enlarged, swiping two fingers across the screen allows you to move around the page to see portions of it that may now be off screen.

✔ **Font Size:** Toggles on and off larger fonts onscreen.

✔ **Closed Captioning:** Turns on closed captioning for videos; note that only some videos are enabled for closed captioning.

✔ **Closed Captioning Preferences:** Allows you to choose settings such as caption text size, color, and font, as well as the text background color.

✔ **Convert Stereo to Mono:** If you have poor hearing in one ear, stereo sound can make you miss some of the audio coming at you. You can use this setting to turn on Mono audio.

✔ **Accessibility User's Guide:** For a quick tutorial on how to use various accessibility features, tap this and scroll through the user's guide that's displayed.

Making Security & Privacy Settings

The first thing you can do to keep your Fire tablet secure is to avoid letting it out of your hands. But because we can't control everything and sometimes things get lost or stolen, it's a good idea to assign a password that's required to unlock your Fire tablet screen. If other people then get their hands on your Fire, they have no way to get at stored data, such as your Amazon account information or contacts, without knowing the password.

In Settings, tap the Security & Privacy option and you'll see these choices (see Figure 4-7):

✔ **Lock Screen Password:** Simply tap the On button to require that a PIN be used to unlock your device. When you do, fields appear labeled New PIN and Confirm New PIN. Think of a PIN, fill the fields in, and tap Finish to save your new PIN.

✔ **Lock Screen Notifications:** If you want to set a password and still be able to swipe down on the lock screen to view notifications before you enter your password, turn this setting on.

✔ **Credential Storage:** Credentials are typically used for Microsoft Exchange–based accounts, such as an account you use to access email on your company's server. If you use Microsoft Exchange, it's a good idea to get your network administrator's help to make the Trusted Credentials settings.

✔ **Device Administrators:** If your device is being administered through a company Exchange account, use this setting to establish the device administrator who can modify settings for the account.

✔ **Encryption:** To be extra secure, you can set up encryption of the data on your Fire. *Encryption* makes contents unreadable by anybody who doesn't have your password.

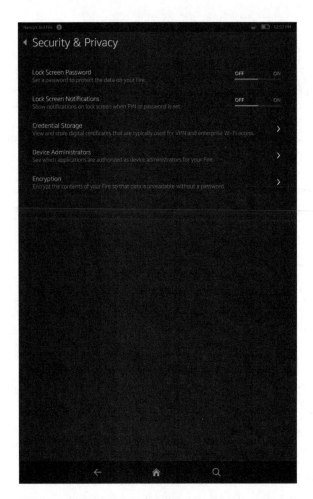

Figure 4-7: The Security settings offer five ways to secure your Fire tablet.

Note that you can also turn on Find Your Tablet through the Device Options settings to enable Amazon to pinpoint a lost Fire. It does so using Location Services, a tracking system that can detect your Fire's location.

To find your lost Fire, follow these steps:

1. **Sign into your Amazon account on another device.**

2. **Choose Manage Your Content and Devices in My Account.**

3. **Tap the Your Devices tab.**

4. **Select a device.**

5. **On the Device Actions drop-down list, choose Find Your Tablet.**

Working with Power-Management Features

With the latest generation of Fire tablets comes a Power Management item in the Settings screen. The first two settings deal with when SmartSuspend kicks in to turn off your network connection.

Two other settings are available in the Power Management settings screen: Display Brightness (a brighter display drains your battery faster) and Wireless settings. You can access both of these through Quick Settings when you first swipe down from the top of your screen, and they're covered in detail in Chapter 3.

SmartSuspend is a new power-management feature. SmartSuspend senses when your tablet hasn't been used for a bit, and disconnects from your network. Because, when you're connected to a network, data may update and download to your device, disconnecting saves battery life.

The first SmartSuspend setting, shown in Figure 4-8, simply turns the feature on or off. With it turned on, the Schedule Wi-Fi Suspend setting becomes available. This setting allows you to schedule suspend times, instead of them happening automatically. Tap Schedule Wi-Fi Suspend to see the screen shown in Figure 4-9.

Use the Duration From/To sliders to set up a time of day for SmartSuspend to kick in. You can also use the Repeat settings beneath the sliders to have the suspend repeat every day, or only on weekdays or weekends. For example, if you sleep late on weekends and you don't want your kids accessing your network from your tablet till 10 a.m., you can set up a repeating suspend on weekends from 5 a.m. till 10 a.m.

When you've finished making settings, tap Set Time to save them.

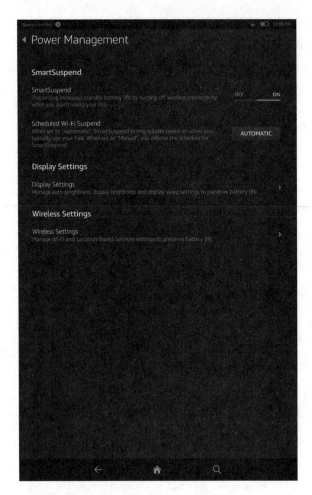

Figure 4-8: Turn on SmartSuspend to save battery life.

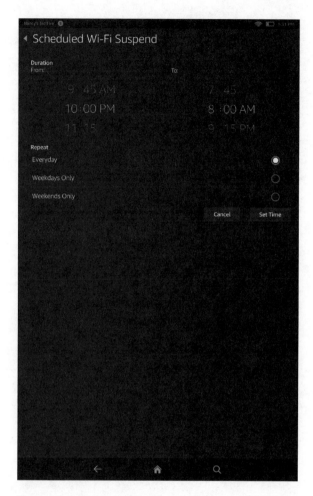

Figure 4-9: Schedule when a suspend will occur with these settings.

5

Fire Tablets and Your Family

*Y*our Fire tablet offers several features that make using it with other family members easy. There's the Fire HD Kids Edition, a new kid-friendly tablet with a free year of FreeTime Unlimited. FreeTime Unlimited (which you can subscribe to from any Fire tablet) offers age-appropriate content and controls.

In addition, you can now create Profiles for each member of your family; with profiles, even if you all share one Fire tablet, it's as if you each had your own version with its own settings. Family Library is a new feature that links accounts so people accessing the library can view all content purchased on that account.

Finally, in this chapter I also cover Parental Controls, built into every Fire tablet; these controls let you manage what kinds of apps and content each of your kids can access.

Scoping Out the Fire HD Kids Edition

New in 2014 is a Fire HD Kids Edition with a rugged case for those tiny hands to grip and several kid-friendly features parents will love. Sporting pink, blue, or green cases, these Fire tablets are geared toward having fun and learning.

Price and replacement guarantee

The Kids Edition has all the basic features of the comparable 6- and 7-inch Fire non-kid tablets, including a quad-core processor and front- and rear-facing cameras. The screen offers high-definition quality, and the Dolby sound makes listening to audiobooks or watching video a great experience.

Besides the rugged case, the Fire HD Kids Edition, priced at $149, has a two-year replacement guarantee. That means that if your child breaks the tablet, it will be replaced without question, which is a pretty sweet deal.

The Kids Edition comes in either 6- or 7-inch versions with 8GB of storage. Each is a fully functioning tablet, though by using Parental Controls (covered later in this chapter), you can set pretty specific limits as to what content, apps, and purchasing power your child has access to.

You might want to consider two accessories that are available from Amazon for the Kids Edition. You can buy the Kids Headphone from Amazon at $29.99 in blue, orange, or purple. The color-matched car charger ($24.99) is great for those long road trips when you want to keep your kids amused for the duration.

Free year of FreeTime Unlimited

FreeTime Unlimited is a subscription service providing age-appropriate content for kids. When you buy a Kids Fire tablet, you get one free year of FreeTime Unlimited. After that, a year's subscription will cost you $4.99 a month for one child or $2.99 a month for Prime members. You can also opt to spend $9.99 a month for up to four children or $6.99 if you have Amazon Prime.

Note that you can subscribe to FreeTime Unlimited on any Fire tablet model and navigate into FreeTime Unlimited with a password so your kids can't open it without your permission, if you like.

FreeTime Unlimited offers about 5,000 kid-friendly books, music, movies, TV shows, educational apps, and games with easy visual navigation. I found two statements from Amazon about the best age range for FreeTime Unlimited: for kids ages 3 to 8 or 3 to 10; however, you should still use your best judgment about your own child's interests and maturity.

FreeTime Unlimited, shown in Figure 5-1, has fun background colors and fonts that appeal to younger kids. In addition, FreeTime Unlimited has no ads and no in-app purchases.

Coming soon is a FreeTime Unlimited camera and photo apps with some fun editing tools. Parents can even print out their kids' art and hang it in the appropriate spot on the refrigerator or wall.

If your family members devour lots of content, consider paying $9.99 a month for Kindle Unlimited. With this subscription, you can pick and choose from over 700,000 book titles and thousands of audiobooks.

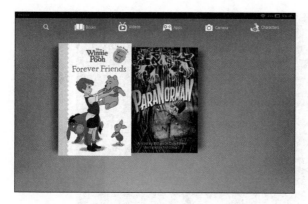

Figure 5-1: FreeTime has a unique interface younger kids will appreciate.

Setting Up Profiles

The ability to set up Profiles, new with the 2014 Fire tablets, means that you can devise a specific Fire experience for up to six people with unique access to content, the built-in cameras, and other settings. You can create up to two adult profiles and four children's profiles and manage each child's permissions.

When you set up a profile, you add a person to your Household. Members of your Household can use the content sharing features of Family Library, covered in the "Using Family Library," later in this chapter.

To set up a new adult profile, follow these steps:

1. **Swipe down from the top of the screen and tap Settings.**

   The Settings screen appears.

2. **Tap Profiles & Family Library.**

   If requested enter your password. All existing profiles are listed on this screen and tap Submit.

3. **Tap Add Adult.**

   A message appears asking you to pass the tablet to the person you want to add.

   The screen shown in Figure 5-2 appears.

4. **The person being added should select whether he has his own account, or if he needs to create an account to use for this profile.**

   The rest of these steps assume the person has an Amazon account; if not, just choose the option that the person needs to create an account and follow prompts to create the profile.

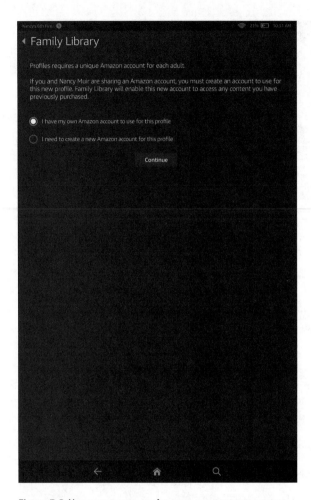

Figure 5-2: You can create an Amazon account now or use an existing one.

5. **Tap Continue.**

6. **The new user should enter an email address and password for the account.**

   On the next screen, that person is asked if he wants to share purchases (see Figure 5-3).

7. **The person should tap the items he wants to share, and then tap Continue.**

   Fire prompts the new user to hand the device back to its owner.

8. Tap Continue.

9. On the following screen, choose Enable Content Sharing, and tap Continue.

10. On the following screen, tap the items to share and then tap Continue.

    The confirmation screen appears.

11. Tap OK to finish the setup.

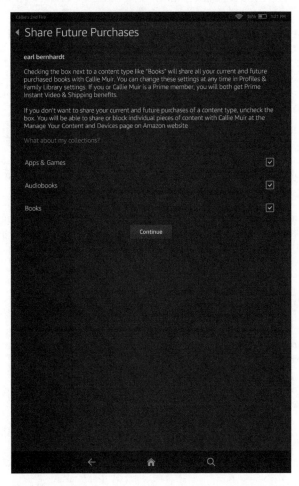

Figure 5-3: When creating an adult profile, choose what to share with the device owner here.

To create a child's profile is a bit simpler, though after you do, you have more settings available to control that child's online experience. To create a child profile, follow these steps:

1. **From the Profiles & Family Library, tap Add Child.**

2. **Enter a name, and then use the next two drop-down lists to choose the child's gender and birthdate.**

   These settings will come into play to manage available content if your child uses the FreeTime Unlimited feature, covered in the next task.

3. **You can also tap the Set Photo picture placeholder and choose a provided image or tap Use a Photo to select a photo stored on your Fire tablet.**

4. **Tap Create Profile.**

   You're presented with a list of apps that you own that would be age appropriate for the profile you just created.

5. **Tap titles you want available to your child, and then tap Done.**

See "Working with Parental Controls" in this chapter for more about how to block, unblock, and password-protect access to content on the tablet your child uses.

After you set up some profiles, you can sign into one from the Lock screen. Tap the owner's profile in the top-left corner, tap the individual profile you want to sign on with, and then swipe the arrow on the right side to log in as that person.

Exploring FreeTime Unlimited

When you have FreeTime Unlimited and you've set up your child's profile (see the previous task), you can access FreeTime by tapping the FreeTime app in the Apps library or Carousel.

Here's a quick run-through of FreeTime Unlimited's key features. With FreeTime you can

- ✔ Set daily limits and a specific bedtime after which the child can't use FreeTime.

- ✔ Block access to games and cartoons until after educational goals are reached.

- ✔ Restrict access to games and video but leave reading wide open.

From the FreeTime Home screen, recent content is displayed on a central Carousel, just as on the regular Fire tablet Home screen. Your child can tap a category such as Books to see a selection of content that's appropriate to the age in the child's profile. You can tap Characters to see collections of content related to characters, such as Sesame Street, dinosaurs, or Disney.

To make settings for this child's FreeTime usage, swipe down from the top of the screen in FreeTime and tap Settings. Enter your passcode and tap Submit to access FreeTime Settings, shown in Figure 5-4. Tap a setting such as Set Daily Goals and Time Limits and choose which child you want to make these settings for. Swipe to turn the feature on and you'll see the settings shown in Figure 5-5.

Without the password, your child has no access to FreeTime settings and settings such as connecting to a wireless network.

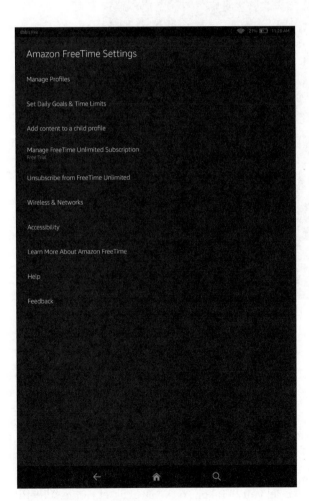

Figure 5-4: Choose a setting to modify here.

Figure 5-5: Control what you do and don't want your child to do and for how long.

If you choose the Add Content to a Child Profile setting on the screen shown in Figure 5-4, you can then tap a child's profile and add Amazon titles (apps, videos, and books) to your child's FreeTime libraries. Amazon preselects those that should be age appropriate, but you can tap to deselect any you don't want to add. This is also the place where you can manage or cancel your subscription to FreeTime.

To exit FreeTime, swipe down and tap Exit Profile, tap your own profile, and enter your passcode; you're taken to the Fire tablet Home screen.

That gives you an overview of FreeTime. If you have a Kids Fire tablet, FreeTime Unlimited is free for a year, so explore it to your heart's content.

Using Family Library

Family Library is a feature that was announced but isn't yet available at the time of this writing. As Amazon describes it, this feature allows you to add people to your Household so they can share content purchased with a single account and credit card among various Fire devices. That means that if you buy a book on your Fire and your husband or child wants to read it on theirs, assuming that person is a member of your Household, he or she can simply read it from their Fire tablet.

When you add a profile to your Fire, that person is automatically added to your Household, which can include up to two adults and four children.

You may want to remove somebody from your Household — maybe your son who just graduated from college. Just swipe down from the top of the screen and tap Settings⇨Profiles & Family Library. Tap a profile. Tap Remove from Household and then tap Remove Profile.

You can't recover a profile once it's deleted from your Household; you'll have to create the profile all over again.

If your family includes college-aged kids, you'll be delighted to know that they can rent etextbooks for about a quarter of the price of printed versions, and buy etextbooks for about half the price of the print books. If you include your kids in your Family Library, you can see what they're learning.

Working with Parental Controls

Parental Controls allow you to make settings to block or unblock or password-protect certain kinds of content and features.

When you turn on the Parental Controls setting, you're first presented with the fields for entering and confirming a password. When you've entered your password, tap Finish. Note that once you have created this password, whenever you go into Parental Controls and enter that password, you tap Submit to proceed.

When you create a child's profile or turn on Parental Controls, you are then required to enter a password every time you want to open your tablet from the Lock screen.

In the following screen (see Figure 5-6), you can access children's profiles (see the earlier task, "Setting Up Profiles," for more about the Profiles feature).

Beneath that setting, you tap to turn Parental Controls on or off. With it on, you see settings to block or unblock the Web Browser; Email, Contacts, and Calendars; Social Sharing; Camera; Amazon Maps; Firefly; and Amazon Stores. For example, if you don't want your child to use email or take photos yet, block them. As your child gets older, you can unblock and give access to more apps and features.

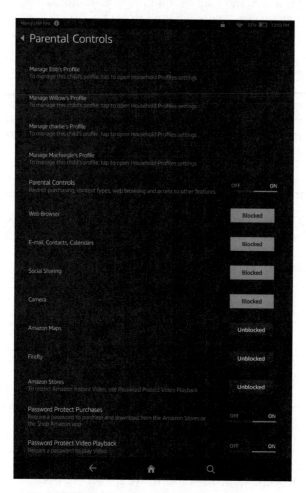

Figure 5-6: Choose what to block or unblock here.

You can also tap to password-protect purchases or video playback. Why you'd want to avoid allowing your child to buy what she likes from Amazon is probably obvious. Password-protecting video protects your kids from undesirable video content, and saves your tablet's battery life from the drain of constantly streaming video.

If you want to allow or block certain types of content such as books or photos, tap Block and Unblock Content Types. On the list of content types that appears, tap to block content such as Music or Audiobooks.

Back in the Parental Controls screen, the final settings concern the password for your device. Tap Change Password to go to another screen, where you can create a new password you use to open your tablet from the Lock screen, or use the Off/On switches in the next three settings to password-protect the following:

- ✓ **Wi-Fi.** If you block your child from using Wi-Fi, she won't be able to use any content stored in Amazon Cloud Drive or use the Silk web browser. Your child is pretty much limited to content and apps you've down-loaded to the device.

- ✓ **Location-Based Services.** If you block this feature, it limits the useful-ness of apps, such as Weather or Maps, that rely on being able to iden-tify your location to provide accurate information. However, the upside is that other people your child encounters online can't use location-based services in places such as Facebook to spot where your child is. Some use it for the purposes of ID theft (because they know both a name and town where the child lives) or to make unwelcome offline contact.

- ✓ **Mayday.** This live Help feature is great for getting support for your Fire tablet. However, the helpful folks at Amazon probably don't want your 4-year-old constantly tapping Mayday (only available on the 8.9-inch model of Fire) to chat with a person about non-Fire–related stuff. If your child has discovered Mayday and become addicted to it, you can block his access to the feature here.

If you turn on location-based services, you're sharing very private informa-tion about your whereabouts. If you're concerned about what apps have access to your location, check out those apps in the Amazon Appstore to see whether the permissions listed on their details pages mention use of location information.

Part II
Taking the Leap Online

In this part . . .

- ✔ Shop for apps in the Amazon Appstore.
- ✔ Browse the Internet.
- ✔ Set up your email account.

6

Going Shopping

In This Chapter

▶ Using your Amazon account

▶ Shopping at the Amazon Appstore

▶ Buying apps, music, video, and printed publications

▶ Buying other Amazon items through your Fire tablet

*B*ecause your Fire tablet is, above all, a great device for consuming content (especially Amazon-provided content), knowing how to buy that content or download free content is key to enjoying it. Amazon offers a rich supply of books, magazines, music, and video as well as an Appstore that you can use to get your hands on apps that add to the functionality of your Fire tablet. These apps can range from simple accessories such as a notes program to fun and addictive games and maps programs.

In this chapter, you discover how to get apps as well as books, magazines, music, audiobooks, and videos for your Fire tablet.

Managing Your Amazon Account

You buy things from Amazon by using the account and payment information you provide when you create an Amazon account. You probably have an account if you ever bought anything on Amazon.

To open an account, you should go to www.amazon.com, and when you attempt to purchase something, you'll be asked for your Amazon credentials. Tap the No, I Am a New Customer option and follow the steps to obtain your account credentials.

To buy things on Amazon with your Fire tablet, you need to have registered your Fire tablet using an Amazon account, which usually happens during the setup process, covered in Chapter 2. You can change the account to which your tablet is registered by deregistering it and then registering it to the Amazon credentials for the other account. For example, if you prefer to have purchases charged to your spouse's Amazon account or you are giving or selling your Fire to somebody else, you might want to associate it with a different Amazon account. You can do this by following these steps:

1. **Swipe down from the top of the screen to display Quick Settings.**

2. **Tap Settings.**

3. **Tap My Account (see Figure 6-1).**

4. **Tap the Deregister button.**

   A confirming screen appears.

5. **Tap Deregister.**

6. **Tap the Register button.**

7. **Enter your preferred Amazon credentials (email address and a password) for the account you want to associate with your device.**

8. **Tap Create Account.**

After you associate your device with an Amazon account, you can manage account settings and payment options by following these steps:

1. **Navigate to the Amazon website** (www.amazon.com) **by using the browser on either your Fire tablet or your computer.**

2. **Tap (if you're using a touchscreen device) or click Your Account in the top-right corner of the Amazon screen. See Figure 6-2.**

3. **Tap Account in the menu that appears.**

4. **Tap or click the Manage Payment Options from the Payment section of your account.**

   The Credit and Debit Cards page appears. If you want to add a new payment method at this point, choose Add Credit/ Debit Card.

5. **Click a payment method and make changes using the Delete or Edit button.**

   Your changes are automatically saved. Now when you purchase items from your Amazon Fire tablet, the default payment and billing option is used to complete the purchase.

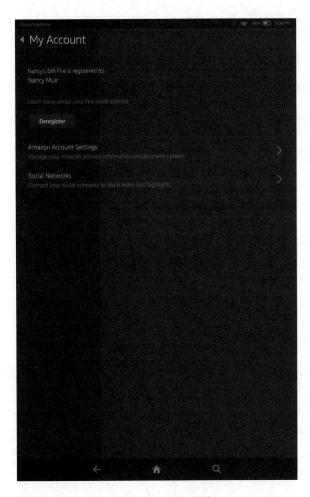

Figure 6-1: Deregister your account on this screen.

Figure 6-2: Managing your Amazon account on a PC.

Visiting the Amazon Appstore

After you register your Amazon account with your Fire tablet (which I discuss in the preceding section), you can start shopping for all kinds of content. I start by introducing you to the world of apps.

Apps provide you with functionality of all kinds, from an app that turns your Fire tablet into a star-gazing tool to game apps. You can find acupuncture apps, drawing apps, and apps that provide maps so that you can find your way in the world.

Exploring the world of apps

You can buy apps for your Fire tablet by using the Amazon Appstore. This store is full of apps written especially for devices that are based on the Android platform, including Fire tablets.

Android devices may have slightly different operating systems, and therefore not every app will work on every device. See Chapter 14 for some suggested apps that will work well with your Fire tablet.

Follow these steps to explore the world of apps:

1. **Tap the Apps button at the top of the Fire Home screen to enter your Apps library.**

2. **Tap the Store button.**

   The Appstore appears (see Figure 6-3).

Apps can be addictive; just be sure you don't glut your Fire tablet's memory with free or for-a-price apps you're not really going to use.

Swipe upward to scroll down the page to view recommendations for you in categories such as games or free apps. You can tap See More to reveal more apps in each category. Tap the Left Nav button in the top-left corner to display the Navigation panel. From here you can select categories of apps such as Games, Best Sellers, and New Releases.

Tap Browse Categories in the Navigation panel to see a list of all categories of apps such as Entertainment and Cooking; then tap a category to go there.

Figure 6-3: The Amazon Appstore.

Searching for apps

You can have fun browsing through categories of apps and recommendations, but if you know which app you want to buy, using the Search feature can take you right to it.

To search for an app, follow these steps:

1. **Tap in the Search button in the Appstore. See Figure 6-4.**

   The keyboard shown in Figure 6-5 appears.

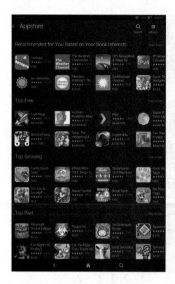
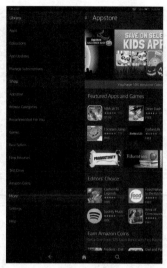

Figure 6-4: Get recommendations and view categories of apps by using the Navigation panel.

2. **Using the onscreen keyboard, enter the name of an app, such as Angry Birds.**

   Suggested matches to the search term appear beneath the Search field.

3. **Tap a suggested search term to display a list of detailed results.**

4. **Tap an app name in the results to see an app description page.**

   The Product Info screen appears. Read the description and scroll down to read customer reviews or explore other apps that customers who bought this app also bought.

Buying apps

You can use your Amazon account payment option to buy apps, or you can use Amazon Coins, a feature that lets you buy apps and games with prepaid credits. When you use Coins, you can get savings in prices — as much as 10 percent. When you buy a new Fire tablet, it comes with 500 coins, which is about $5 in real money. I tell you more about using the Coins in the upcoming steps.

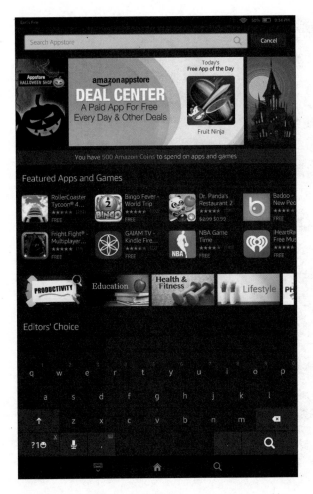

Figure 6-5: Use the search field and onscreen keyboard in the Appstore to find what you want.

Whether you find something you want to own by browsing or searching, when you're ready to buy, you can follow these steps:

1. **From the app's Product Info screen (see the preceding section), tap the Price button. See Figure 6-6.**

   Note that if the app is free, this button reads Free, but if you have to pay for the app, the app price (such as $0.99 or 99 coins) is displayed on the button. When you tap the button for a paid item, a dialog box appears with a link to Buy More coins (or use existing coins if you have enough) or purchase with your Amazon account 1-Click payment method.

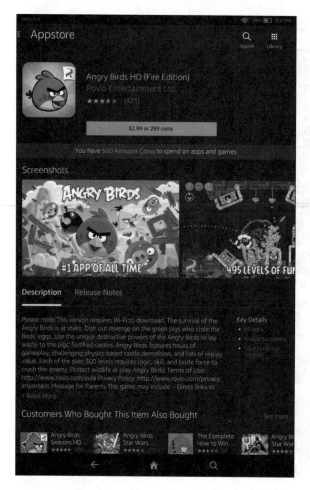

Figure 6-6: Product details are shown in the Product Info screen.

2. **Tap the Buy Now button to download paid apps. Tap Get App to download free apps. See Figure 6-7.**

   A Downloading button appears, showing the download progress. When the installation is complete, an Open button appears.

3. **If you want to use the app immediately, tap the Open button.**

To use the app at any time, locate it in the app library or, if you've used it recently, on the Carousel; tap the app to open it. Each app has its own controls and settings, so look for a Settings menu like the one for the Solitaire game shown in Figure 6-8.

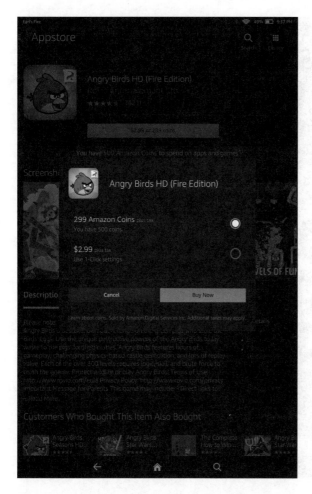

Figure 6-7: Tap Buy Now or Get App to make the app your own.

You can also buy apps from Amazon on your PC or Mac. When placing the app in your shopping cart, be sure to select your Fire tablet for the device you want to download the app to in the drop-down list below the Add to Cart button. When you complete your purchase, assuming that you're in range of a Wi-Fi network, the app is immediately downloaded to your Fire tablet.

To delete an installed app from your App library, press and hold it until a menu appears and then tap Remove. In the drop-down menu that appears, tap From Device. The app, however, isn't gone — it's still stored in the Amazon Cloud Drive, and you can download it again at any time by tapping it in the Cloud tab of the App library.

Figure 6-8: App settings for Solitaire.

Buying Content

Apps and games are great, but shopping for content is my favorite thing to do. I'm not putting down games and financial apps, but to me, content means a night at the movies, a rainy afternoon with a good book, or a relaxing hour listening to a soothing collection of music.

From Amazon, you can buy publications, books, music, audiobooks, and video (movies and TV shows) to download or stream to your Fire tablet. The buying process is somewhat similar for the different types of content, but there are slight variations, which I go into in the following sections.

Buying publications through Newsstand

There's a world of periodicals out there, from magazines to newspapers, just waiting for you to explore them. Your Fire tablet's display makes browsing through color magazines especially appealing.

Tap Newsstand on the Home screen and then tap the Store button to see several categories of items (see Figure 6-9).

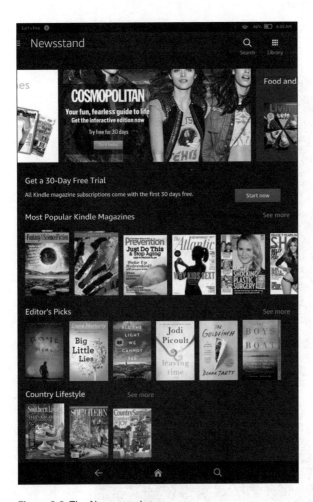

Figure 6-9: The Newsstand store.

You'll see categories such as Most Popular Kindle Magazines and Featured Newspapers. Swipe right to left to scroll through each category.

Scroll down to see categories such as Sports & Outdoors and Family & Parenting (though the categories change on a regular basis). You can tap the See More button to the right and above any category to see a more complete list of included items.

When you find the publication you want, follow these steps to buy or subscribe to it:

1. **Tap the item.**

   A screen appears showing pricing, a description of the publication, and Subscribe Now, Try FREE, or Buy Issue buttons (see Figure 6-10).

Figure 6-10: Details about a publication and buttons to help you purchase or subscribe.

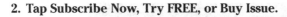

2. **Tap Subscribe Now, Try FREE, or Buy Issue.**

The button label changes to read Downloading and your free 30-day sub-scription begins; when it's completed, the item is charged to your Amazon account payment method. During the download process, you can tap the Cancel button if you change your mind. When the download is complete, the button label changes to Read Now.

3. **Tap the Read Now button to open the magazine.**

Note that the magazine is stored in your Amazon Cloud library, where you can read or download it to your Fire tablet via Newsstand at a later time.

You can tap the Left Nav button and choose from the many categories listed there to find your publication of choice, or tap the Search button on any screen to search for a particular publication.

Buying books

I may be partial to books because I write them, but I hardly think I'm alone. If you've joined the electronic book revolution (or even if you haven't), you'll find that reading books on your Fire tablet is convenient and economical (ebooks are typically a few dollars less than the print version, and you can borrow many ebooks from your local library for free).

To browse through ebooks from Amazon on your Fire tablet, follow these steps:

1. **Tap the Books button on the Fire tablet Home screen.**

2. **Tap the Store button.**

The Amazon Bookstore sports a Recommended for You section near the top that suggests books for you based on your buying history.

3. **Swipe right to left to scroll through the recommendations.**

You also see categories such as Kindle Daily Deals, New & Noteworthy, and Best Sellers.

As with the Newsstand, when you locate and tap an item in the bookstore, you see a screen with that item's pricing and description (see Figure 6-11). In the bookstore, the buttons vary, and could include Borrow for Free, Download Sample, Buy, Buy for Free, and More Options.

To use any buying option, you must have set up 1-Click settings for your Amazon account, which you can do by going to Amazon.com and modifying your payment methods.

Figure 6-11: Details about a book in the Amazon Bookstore.

Here's how these three buttons work:

- **Download a Sample:** Tap this button, and it changes to a Downloading button and then to a Read Now button. Tap the Read Now button to open the sample of the book.

- **Buy or Buy for Free:** Tap this button, and it changes to a Downloading button. When the download is complete, the button label changes to Read Now. Tap the Read Now button to open the book. Remember that the book is now stored in your Books library, where you can tap it to open and read it at your leisure. Some books also offer a Borrow for Free button for Prime members only.

✔ **More Options:** This button offers two options, Add to Wish List and Print Editions From, with the price showing on the right of the button. Tap Add to Wish List so that you can easily find it again in the Navigation panel of the store to buy it at a later date. Tap Print Editions From to add the item to your Amazon shopping cart and specify shipping information.

The sample or purchased book appears in your Books library, which you reach by tapping Books from the Home screen and then tapping the Library button (on the Carousel on the Fire Home screen).

To remove a book from your device (remembering that it will be stored in the Amazon Cloud if you purchased it), open your Books library, press and hold the book image, tap Remove at the top right of the screen, and then tap From Device.

For more about reading ebooks and periodicals on your Fire, see Chapter 8.

Buying music

You may hate computer games, and you might not read books very often, but I've never met anybody who doesn't like some kind of music. No matter what kind of music you prefer, from hip-hop to Broadway, you're likely to find a great many selections tucked away in Amazon's vaults.

Tap the Music button on the Fire tablet Home screen and then tap the Store button. Near the middle of the screen, you'll see Songs Recommended for You (see Figure 6-12). These are based on music you've previously purchased. You can also scroll down the screen and tap categories such as Featured Albums and Latest in Prime to view music by these criteria.

All over the Music store home page, you'll see thumbnails of music selections.

Follow these steps to buy music:

1. **Tap an item.**

   A screen appears, displaying a list of the songs in the case of an album with Price buttons for both the entire album and each individual song.

2. **Tap the icon to the left of a song to play a preview of it.**

3. **Tap a Buy Album For button, with the price of the album also displayed on the button.**

   The button label changes from the price of the item to the words Buy Now.

4. **Tap the Buy Now button.**

   The song or album downloads to your Music library. A confirmation screen appears, displaying a See Album in Library button and a Continue Shopping button (see Figure 6-13).

Figure 6-12: The Amazon Music store.

5. **Tap the See Album in Library button to open the album and display the list of songs.**

   The first time you download music, you may be asked to choose whether you want content automatically downloaded to your device when you buy it. When you download an album, it's stored both in your Music library and the Amazon Cloud Drive. If you tap a song to play it, it'll also appear with recently accessed content in the Carousel.

   If you tap the Continue Shopping button, you can later find the album in your Music library.

   See Chapter 9 for more about playing music.

Figure 6-13: This dialog box allows you to return to your library or keep shopping.

Buying video

You should definitely check out the experience of consuming a downloaded video program from your Fire tablet. From lying in bed or on the beach to watching your videos while waiting in line at the bank, portability can be a very convenient feature.

When you tap Videos on the Fire tablet Home screen, you're instantly taken to the Amazon Video Store, shown in Figure 6-14.

Across the middle of the screen, you see thumbnails of items recommended based on what you've watched, followed by items recently added to the Prime Instant Videos inventory. You can also scroll down to view shows that offer a First Episode Free so that you can sample shows that are new to you.

Figure 6-14: Shop for video in the Amazon Video Store.

Tap an item in any category, and a descriptive screen appears. For TV shows, this screen includes episode prices for TV shows and a Season button that displays a drop-down list to switch to another season. For movies, this screen may include Watch Trailer, Buy, and Rent buttons (see Figure 6-15). You can also scroll down and view details about the movie's director, release year, and more.

Tap a Buy or Rent button with the price on it (such as Rent HD $5.99), and it becomes a confirming Buy or Rent button (such as Rent HD), depending on which transaction you select. Tap this button, and your purchase or rental is processed.

When you tap a Rent button you're immediately charged for the rental. The rental period begins when you start to watch the movie.

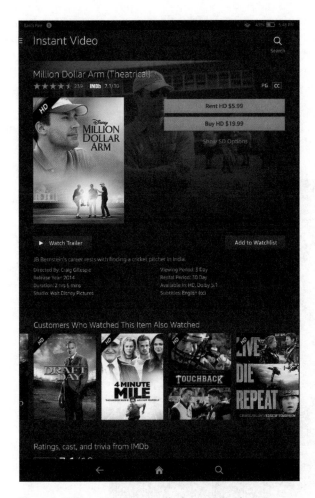

Figure 6-15: The video screen offers several options.

See Chapter 10 for more about playing videos.

If you tap the Add to Watchlist button, the item is added to your watchlist so that you can find it easily to rent or buy it at some future time. To view your Watchlist, tap the Left Nav button when in the Videos library or store and then tap Your Watchlist. Tap any item in the watchlist to open a screen similar to the one shown in Figure 6-15.

Shopping for Anything Else

Amazon kindly pre-installed an Amazon Shopping app on your Fire tablet so that you can quickly go to their online store and buy anything your heart desires.

The Amazon Shopping app (see Figure 6-16) is included with your Fire tablet right out of the box. Just tap Shop from the Fire tablet Home screen and then tap Shop Amazon. Amazon opens in your browser with a list of recommendations for you, based on previous purchases. You can shop by department from the list of available departments.

Now, just proceed to shop as you usually do on Amazon, tapping any item of interest to add it to your cart and using your Amazon account information to pay and arrange for shipping.

Figure 6-16: Tap the Shop Amazon app to go shopping for virtually anything.

7

Going Online

*Y*ears ago, the best way to stay in touch with the outside world was by reading the morning paper and going to the mailbox to get your mail. Today, browsing the web and checking email has replaced this routine in many of our lives. Your Fire tablet can become your new go-to device for keeping informed and in touch by using Amazon's Silk browser and the pre-installed email client.

In this chapter, you discover the ins and outs of browsing with Silk and the simple tools you can use to send and receive email on your Fire tablet.

Getting Online by Using Wi-Fi

Unless you own a 4G LTE version of the Fire tablet, your Fire is a Wi-Fi–only device, meaning that you have to connect to a nearby Wi-Fi network to go online. You might access a Wi-Fi connection through your home network, at work, or via a public hotspot, such as an Internet cafe or airport.

When you first set up your Fire tablet (as described in Chapter 2), you can choose a Wi-Fi network to use for going online. If you want to log on to a different network, follow these steps:

1. **Swipe down from the top of the Home screen to display Quick Settings, which reveals a menu of common settings, such as Quiet Time, Wireless, and Brightness.**

2. **Tap Wireless.**

   Wireless settings appear (see Figure 7-1).

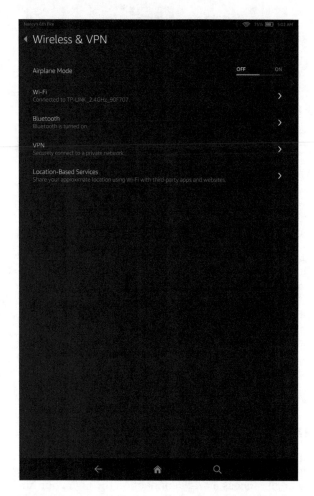

Figure 7-1: Wireless settings allow you to select an available network to join.

3. **Tap Wi-Fi.**

4. **Tap a network in the list of available wireless networks, enter a password, and then tap Connect to sign in.**

You have to enter a password to sign in to some networks. If you're already connected to a network when you tap its name here, you get information about the connection (the signal strength, link speed, and so on). You also can tap a Forget button to lose your connection to it.

Browsing the Internet with Silk

Silk is a browser created by Amazon. Some people wondered why Amazon didn't choose to use an existing browser, such as Internet Explorer, for the Fire tablet. The answer is that Silk takes advantage of Amazon's ability to use its own servers to make your browsing experience fast.

For example, if you visit a popular news website and choose to tap the headline story to get more details, the odds are that many thousands of people have done the same thing. The Silk browser recognizes this pattern and holds that next page in its *cache* (a dedicated block of memory) to deliver it quickly to you if you also make this selection. This ability is supposed to make your browsing experience as fast and smooth as, well, silk.

Silk offers several features for more user-friendly or speedier browsing. Reading View allows you to view content without the typical distracting web-page chaos such as ads. The navigation panel that slides out on the left of the screen offers shortcuts to content such as Most Visited and Bookmarks. These selections make it simpler to find pages in a neat grid pattern of thumbnails.

In the following sections, I introduce you to Silk's browser environment. Many tools and features will be familiar to you from other browsers, but a few are unique to Silk.

Getting around

From the Fire tablet's Home screen, tap the Web button to display the Silk browser. You can also reach Silk by tapping the Silk Browser thumbnail in the Favorites grid at the bottom of your Home screen.

You can navigate among web pages, as shown in Figure 7-2. You can do the following:

Figure 7-2: Silk offers a familiar browser interface.

✔ Use the Back and Forward buttons on the Options bar to move among pages you've viewed.

✔ To search for a page, tap the Search button on the Options bar, enter a site address or search term using the onscreen keyboard, and then tap Go. Results of the search are displayed.

✔ Tap the Menu button (it looks like three dots stacked on top of each other) and tap the Full Screen option to remove the address bar from the screen for easier reading.

✔ Tap the Menu button to add a bookmark or share the page with others via Email, Facebook, Twitter, or Skype (more about these features in later sections of this chapter). Note that if you're on a page that is already bookmarked, the item in the menu reads Edit Bookmark.

Displaying tabs

Silk uses tabs that allow you to display more than one web page at a time and move among those pages. Follow these steps to add a tab:

1. **Tap the Add button in the top-right corner — which looks like a plus sign (+) — to add a tab in the browser.**

   A list of most visited sites appears.

2. **Tap an item in the list, or tap in the Search bar that appears and enter a URL by using the onscreen keyboard; then tap Go on the keyboard.**

   You are taken to that site.

Turning on Reading View

When you're in a view that contains content such as an article, you can turn on the new Reading View to remove clutter from the screen and focus on the text. Reading View hides both the address bar and ads, as well as most images from the article.

To turn Reading View on:

1. **Navigate to a page with an article displayed.**

   For example, Amazon.com, a retail site, won't offer Reading View but CNN.com, a news site, will.

2. **Locate the article you want to read and tap within it.**

3. **Tap the green Reading View button to the right of the address bar.**

   The article text appears and web page clutter goes away (see Figure 7-3).

4. **Tap the Close button in the upper-right of the article to close Reading View.**

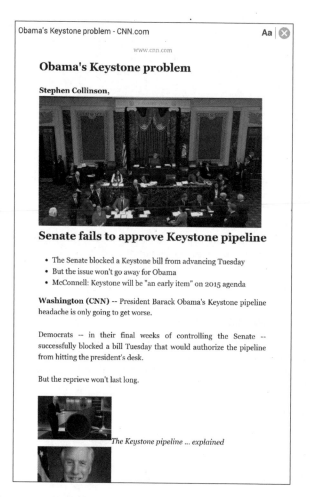

Figure 7-3: This cleaner view of your article is much easier to read.

Bookmarking sites

You can bookmark sites in Silk so that you can easily jump back to them again. Here are the steps to add a Bookmark for a displayed page:

1. **With a site displayed on screen, tap the Menu button in the Options bar (refer to Figure 7-2).**

   The menu shown in Figure 7-4 appears.

2. **Tap Bookmark and then tap the Add button.**

   The Add Bookmark dialog box appears.

3. **If you want, you can enter a new name in the Name field.**

4. **Tap OK.**

   The currently displayed page is bookmarked and the dialog box closes.

5. **Tap the Left Nav button on the top left of the screen to display the Navigation panel.**

6. **Tap Bookmarks and then tap a bookmarked site's thumbnail (see Figure 7-5) to go there.**

Figure 7-4: Bookmarks help you quickly return to a favorite page.

To delete a bookmark, after displaying thumbnails of bookmarked pages, press and hold a page. In the menu that appears, tap Delete. In the confirming dialog box that appears, tap OK and the bookmark is removed.

Figure 7-5: Choose your bookmarked site from this page.

Using web content shortcuts

Silk contains a handy panel of shortcuts you can access from any page. In addition to Help and Settings for Silk, this panel, shown in Figure 7-6, provides shortcuts to

- Most Visited sites
- Bookmarks
- Downloads
- History of your browsing
- Trending Now news stories

To use this panel, follow these steps:

1. **Tap the Left Nav button in the top-left corner of the Silk screen.**

   The panel shown in Figure 7-6 appears.

2. **Tap an item, such as Trending Now.**

   Thumbnails of hot news stories with descriptive captions appear (see Figure 7-7).

Note that the results will vary depending on what you select in Step 2. For example, History will display a list of items, whereas Bookmarks will display thumbnails of websites.

Figure 7-6: A new panel of shortcuts appears to the left.

Figure 7-7: Trending news stories keep you up to date.

Choosing Silk's General settings

At the bottom of the Navigation panel described in the previous section is a Settings button. When you tap that button, you can choose the following General settings (note that Saved Data settings are covered in the later section, "Choosing Privacy Settings"):

- **Search Engine:** Tap this setting to go to a dialog box where you can choose Bing, Google, or Yahoo! as your default search engine.

- **Block Pop-Up Windows:** Some sites generate pop-up windows, some of which are useful and many of which are just annoying ads. Tap this setting and select Ask, Never, or Always to control how and when pop-ups appear on web pages.

✓ **Cloud Features:** Choosing this option allows Amazon to use the Amazon Cloud to make your browsing speed faster, provide support for Flash video, and access sophisticated streaming technology.

✓ **Optional Encryption:** When you browse, requests for page content go through servers, either those used by the page owner or Amazon's. To protect this information, you can encrypt it by turning on Optional Encryption. Be aware, however, that turning this feature on may slow down your browsing experience slightly.

✓ **Enable Instant Page Loads:** If you turn off Accelerate Page Loading, this feature also turns off. You *can* leave Accelerate Page Loading on and turn this feature off, however. What this controls is whether Amazon can observe browsing behavior of the population and preload popular content, so if you choose to display it, it displays faster.

Searching for content on a page

Web pages can contain a lot of content, so it's not always easy to find the article or discussion you want to view on a particular topic. Most browsers provide a feature to search for content on a web page, and Silk is no exception.

To search the currently displayed page by using Silk, follow these steps:

1. **Tap Menu on the Options bar.**

2. **In the list of options that appears (see Figure 7-8), tap Find in Page.**

   The onscreen keyboard appears with the Search field active.

3. **Type a search term.**

   The first instance of a match for the search term on the page appears in an orange highlight. Subsequent instances of the word on that page are highlighted in yellow, as shown in Figure 7-9.

4. **Tap any of the highlighted words that are links to view the related content.**

5. **Tap Done to close the keyboard and end the search.**

Searching the web

Most of us spend a lot of our time online browsing around to find what we want. Search engines make our lives easier because they help us narrow down what we're looking for by using specific search terms; they then troll the web to find matches for those terms from a variety of sources.

Figure 7-8: Search the currently displayed page.

To search the entire web, follow these steps:

1. **Tap the Search button in the Options bar (refer to Figure 7-2).**

   The onscreen keyboard appears.

2. **Enter a search term.**

   Search term matches are listed (see Figure 7-10).

3. **Tap Go on the keyboard.**

   A page of results on the default search engine is displayed.

4. **Tap a result in the search engine results to go to that page.**

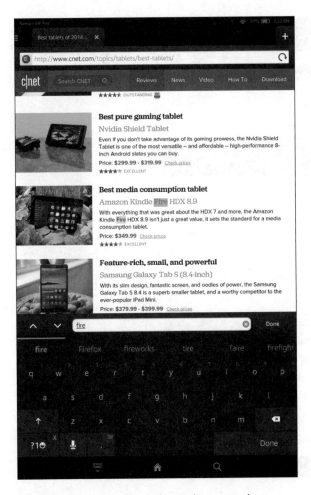

Figure 7-9: The first instance of a word on a page is highlighted in orange.

To specify a search engine to use other than the default, tap the Left Nav button and then tap Settings. Tap the Search Engine option to choose Bing, Google, or Yahoo! as the default search engine.

Reviewing browsing history

We've all experienced this: You know you visited a site in the last day or so that had a great deal, product, news story, or whatever — but you just can't remember the URL of the site. That's where the ability to review your browsing history comes in handy. Using this feature, you can scan the sites you visited recently. They are organized by day, and more often than not, you can spot the place you want to revisit.

Figure 7-10: Search results are displayed in the default search engine you specify — in this case, Bing.

With Silk open:

1. **Tap the Left Nav button.**

2. **Tap History.**

   Sites you've visited on the Fire tablet appear in a list divided into time periods such as Today (see Figure 7-11) and Last 7 Days.

3. **Look over these sites, and when you find the one you want, tap it to go there.**

Figure 7-11: To help you find what you want, sites are divided chronologically.

To avoid losing a site you know you want to revisit, bookmark it using the procedure in the section "Bookmarking sites," earlier in this chapter.

Working with web page content

There are a few things you can do to work with contents of websites using the Silk browser. For example, you may find online content, such as a PDF file, that you want to download to your Docs library, or an image you want to download to the photo gallery. You can also open or share content you find online.

Here's how these features work:

- **View downloads:** Tap the Left Nav button and then tap the Downloads button to view completed downloads.

- **Save or view images:** Press and hold an image, and a menu appears offering options such as Save Image or View Image (see Figure 7-12).

- **Open, save, or share links:** Press and hold your finger on any linked text or image until a menu appears, offering options including Open, Open in New Tab, Open in Background Tab, Bookmark Link, Share Link, Copy Link URL, and Save Link.

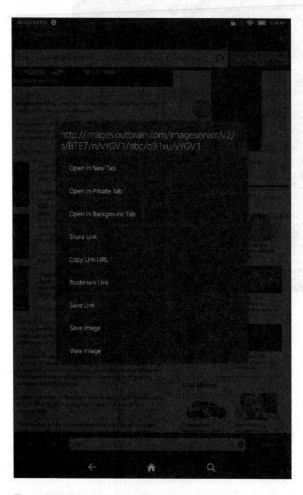

Figure 7-12: You can work with links and images on your Fire tablet by using this menu.

Choosing Privacy Settings

Browsing out there on the Internet can be a bit dangerous. There are people and businesses who want to leave small files on your computer called *cookies* that they use to track your activities or gain illegal access to your online accounts.

Some uses of cookies are perfectly legitimate and allow a reputable business such as Amazon to greet you with personalized recommendations based on your past activities when you visit their sites. Less reputable sites sell your information to others or advertise based on your online history by displaying irritating pop-up windows.

The Privacy settings for Silk help you to stay safe when you're browsing online. With Silk open, tap the Left Nav button and then tap Settings to view and modify the following Saved Data settings (see Figure 7-13):

✔ **Remember Passwords:** This setting saves you the time you'd spend entering usernames and passwords for sites you visit often. Just be aware that this setting puts your accounts at risk should you ever misplace your Fire tablet. One option, if you use this setting, is to require a password to unlock your Fire tablet's Home screen. That setting, which can help protect all content stored on the device, is discussed in Chapter 3.

✔ **Accept Cookies:** Tap this check box to allow sites to download cookies to your Fire tablet.

✔ **Enable Location Access:** Tap this check box to allow websites to request information about your physical location.

✔ **Prompt Before Download:** Turn this feature on to be asked to confirm downloads. This is useful because some sites initiate downloads even if you don't request them, and those downloads could contain malware.

✔ **Clear Browser Data:** Your Silk browser retains a history of your browsing activity to make it easy for you to revisit a site. However, it's possible for others who view your browsing history to draw conclusions about your online habits. To clear your history, tap OK in this setting.

Advanced settings listed below the Saved Data settings allow you to enable or disable JavaScript, which can be used to validate applications, show security warnings, and send requests to websites to not track your activity on them.

If you want to get rid of all the settings you've selected in Silk, with Silk open, tap the Left Nav button and then tap Settings. Scroll down to Advanced Settings and then tap Reset All Settings to Default.

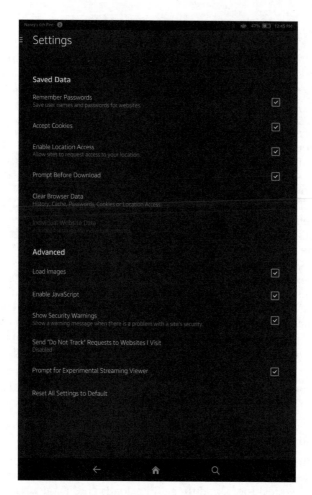

Figure 7-13: Privacy settings can protect your personal information as you browse.

Working with Email

Your Fire tablet has a built-in email client. A *client* essentially allows you to access email accounts you've set up through various providers, such as Gmail and Yahoo!. You can then open the inboxes of these accounts and read, reply to, and forward messages by using your Fire tablet. You can also create and send new messages, and even include attachments.

The latest Email app supports accounts with Outlook, Yahoo!, AOL, and more. You can also group email conversations by subject.

In the following sections, I provide information about setting up and using your email accounts using the Email app on the Fire tablet.

Setting up an email account

Setting up your email on a Fire tablet involves providing information about one or more email accounts that you've already established with a provider, such as Gmail.

Follow these steps to set up an email account the first time you use the app:

1. **Swipe down from the top of the screen and tap Settings.**

2. **Tap Applications⇨Email, Contacts, Calendar.**

   The Email, Contacts, Calendar settings appear.

3. **Tap Add Account.**

4. **Enter your email address and then tap Next.**

   The dialog box shown in Figure 7-14 appears. Note that with certain email accounts, such as Google, this dialog box may sport that service's logo and colors.

5. **Enter your password and then tap Next.**

6. **The Email app verifies your account and displays a Setup Complete screen, where you can choose to go to the email Inbox or add another account.**

Sending email

After you set up your email account(s), as described in the preceding section, you're able to send emails from your Fire tablet. To create and send an email, tap the Email app in the Favorites grid and your email account Inbox opens. Follow these steps to create and send an email:

1. **Tap the New button.**

   A blank email form appears, as shown in Figure 7-15.

2. **In the To field, enter a name.**

   Alternatively, tap the Add Contact button at the far right of the To: field (refer to Figure 7-15) to open the Contacts app and tap a name there to add that person as an addressee (assuming that the Contact record includes an email address).

3. **If you want to send a copy of the email to somebody else, tap the Cc/Bcc button (refer to Figure 7-15) to make those fields appear; then enter addresses or choose them from the Contacts app by tapping the Add Contact button in each field.**

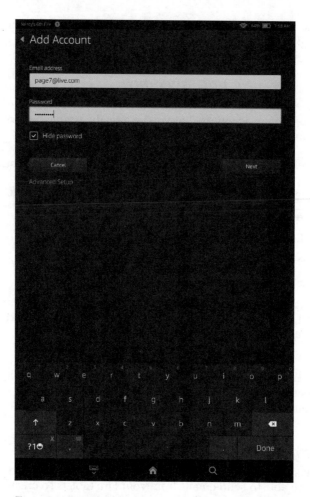

Figure 7-14: Enter the password that goes with your email account here.

4. **Tap in the Subject field and enter a subject by using the onscreen keyboard.**

5. **Tap in the Message text field and enter a message.**

6. **(Optional) If you want to add an attachment to an email, tap the paperclip icon to the right of the Subject field and, in the menu that appears, choose Attach Photo or Attach File. Then choose a file from the sources offered or tap Capture a Photo to snap a photo using your Fire tablet and attach it to your email.**

7. **To send your message, tap the Send button (refer to Figure 7-15).**

    If you decide you're not ready to send the message quite yet, press the back arrow and a draft is automatically saved. You can then tap the Left Nav button, tap Show Folders, and then tap Drafts to view your message drafts.

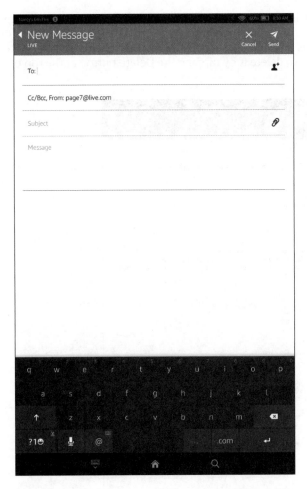

Figure 7-15: A blank form waiting for you to enter an email address, subject, and message.

Here are a couple of handy shortcuts for entering text in your email: The Auto Complete feature lists possible word matches along the top of the onscreen keyboard as you type; tap one to complete a word. In addition, you can double-tap the spacebar to place a period and space at the end of a sentence.

Receiving email

Your Fire tablet can receive your email messages whenever you're connected to a Wi-Fi network. To refresh your inbox so you have access to the most recently received messages, swipe down from the top message in the inbox.

When an email is delivered to your Inbox (see Figure 7-16), simply tap to open it. Read it and contemplate whether you want to save it or delete it (or forward or reply to it, as covered in the following section). If you don't need to keep the message, you can delete it by tapping the Delete button at the top of the screen.

Figure 7-16: Your Inbox.

Forwarding and replying to email

When you receive an email, you can choose to respond to the sender, reply to the sender and anybody else who was included as an addressee on the original message, or forward the email to another person.

If you reply to all recipients, you send an answer to the sender, anybody else in the To field of the original message, and anybody in the Cc and Bcc fields. Because Bcc fields aren't visible to you as a recipient, you may be sending your reply to people you're not aware of.

To forward or reply to an email, with the Email app Inbox displayed, follow these steps:

1. **Tap an email to open it.**

2. **Tap Respond and then tap Reply, Reply All, or Forward (see Figure 7-17).**

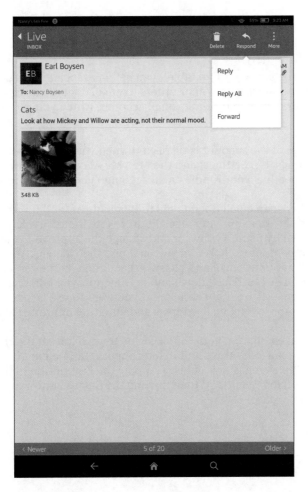

Figure 7-17: Choose to reply to a message or send it on to somebody else.

3. **If you're forwarding the message, enter a new recipient.**

   If you're replying, the message is already addressed, but you can enter additional recipients if you want.

4. **Tap in the message area and enter your message.**

5. **Tap the Send button to send your message on its way.**

When you read a message, you can tell that it has been marked as read when the sender's name is no longer shown in bold. To mark it as unread again, perhaps to draw your attention to it so you read it again, tap the More button in the top-right corner of the screen and then tap the Mark Unread command in the menu that appears.

Sending Email to Your Kindle Account

When you register your Fire tablet, you get an associated email account, which essentially allows you or others to email documents in Word, PDF, RTF, or HTML format to your Kindle email account, which you access on your Fire tablet.

The address of the account is displayed when you swipe down to display Quick Settings, tap Settings, and then tap My Account; you see your name, and underneath is your Kindle email account (*yourname*@kindle.com).

You or others can email documents to this address, and those documents automatically appear in your Docs library. Note that you might need to go to Amazon.com by using a browser and change the approved email accounts. From your computer, click Your Account and then Manage Your Content and Devices. Enter your email and password and then, in the screen that appears, tap the Settings tab. Scroll down and in the Approved Personal Document Email List, make sure that the account you want to use is listed. If it isn't, tap Add a New Approved Email Address and enter the approved email address.

To delete an email from your inbox, swipe toward it from the right side of the screen. Two buttons, Move and Delete, appear. Tap Delete. Note that you can delete multiple emails at a time by tapping the Edit button in the top-right corner, checking items, and then tapping the Delete button that appears at the top of the page.

Part III
Having Fun and Getting Productive

Visit www.dummies.com/extras/firetablets for instructions for inserting objects in WPS Office Word documents.

In this part . . .

✔ Read about using your ereader.

✔ Figure out how to buy and play music.

✔ Use your still camera and video camera.

✔ Engage in social media.

✔ Use Word, Excel, and PowerPoint files.

8

Taking Advantage of the Ereader Extraordinaire

*F*ire tablets come from a family of ereaders, so it's only natural that the ereader you use to read books and magazines on a Fire device is a very robust feature. With its bright, colorful screen, the Fire tablet broadens your reading experience beyond black-and-white books to color publications such as magazines or graphic novels. Its easy-to-use controls help you navigate publications, bookmark and highlight text, and search for text in your books and magazines.

X-Ray is a feature that works with selected books. When a book is X-Ray–enabled, you can view information about characters in the book and jump to locations in the book where those characters appear.

In this chapter, you also discover what's available, how to open publications, and how to read and then delete those publications from your Fire tablet when you're done. You also explore the possibilities of Amazon's lending library and how to lend books to your friends and borrow books from your local public library.

So Many Things to Read!

Amazon started as an online book retailer, although through the years it has branched out to become the largest retailer of just about everything on the planet. The latest Fire tablets make it easy for you to buy content from Amazon. Although you can buy and sideload content from other sources to

Fire tablets, buying from Amazon ensures that you're dealing with a reputable company and receiving safe content (uncontaminated by malware).

The content you buy from Amazon is automatically downloaded to your device, which means that, not only is buying from the Amazon Bookstore easy but also that you can take advantage of its vast selection of books. In addition, you can borrow Kindle versions of books from the Amazon Lending Library as well as from many public libraries. You can also lend books to your friends.

Amazon has also made deals to make many of your favorite magazines and newspapers available. With magazines and newspapers, you can buy a current issue or subscribe to get multiple issues sent to your Fire tablet as they become available.

Goodreads is an app you can download for free that offers a sort of virtual book club. You can share content, reviews, and recommendations with others, and access other peoples' reviews and recommendations. Download the Goodreads app from the Appstore to get started (tap Apps from the Home screen and go to the Store).

Buying books

To buy books or magazines for your Fire tablet, on the Home screen, tap either the Books or Newsstand button, which takes you to your Books or Newsstand library.

Tap the Store button; this takes you to the Amazon Newsstand or Bookstore, shown in Figure 8-1. You can tap the Left Nav button to see a menu of shopping choices such as Browse Categories or Monthly Deals. See Chapter 6 for more about how to search for and buy content.

You can also buy Kindle content from your computer at the Amazon website and have it download to your Fire tablet. Just select what device you want content delivered to from the drop-down list below the Add to Cart button before you buy Kindle content. If you use the Family Library feature, you can share the content you buy with others. See Chapter 5 for more about this.

Amazon uses a technology called Whispersync to allow you to stop reading in one publication on one device and then pick up where you last left off on any devices that use the Kindle ereader app. Whispersync for Voice is a technology that syncs between a printed book and audiobook if you own both. You can leave off reading in the print book, for example, and when you next open your audiobook, it will pick up where you left off reading.

A feature called Matchbook allows you to buy a print edition of a qualifying book and then buy the Kindle version for $2.99 or less. Some books might even be free. This feature can also be applied to all your previous print book purchases.

Figure 8-1: Buy books at the Amazon Bookstore.

Using the Amazon Lending Library

On the screen that appears when you enter the store (see the preceding section), follow these steps to borrow a book:

1. **Tap the Left Nav button.**

2. **Scroll down and tap the Kindle Owners' Lending Library link.**

    A list of free lending selections appears (see Figure 8-2).

These free items are available only if you have an Amazon Prime membership. You get 30 days of Prime free when you buy your Fire tablet.

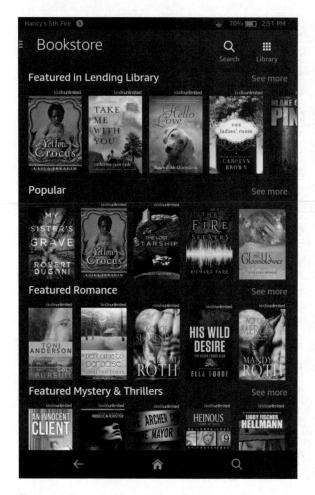

Figure 8-2: These and many more selections are free if you have an Amazon Prime account.

3. **Tap an item to display a description of it.**

4. **Tap the Borrow for Free button.**

   Your selection is immediately downloaded.

You can borrow a title from the Lending Library every 14 days.

If you want to borrow Kindle books on other devices such as your PC, you can do so if you download the Kindle reading app.

For selected titles that you've bought in Kindle format, you can lend them to others for a period of 14 days. Go to the product detail page on Amazon.com and click Loan This Book at the top of the page. On the Loan This Book page, enter an email address for the person you're lending the book to. Enter a personal message if you like, and then click Send Now. Remember, this feature is available only for some books, not all, and you can figure out which books are compliant by looking at the Product Details to see if Lending is enabled. Remember also that a book can only be loaned once.

Borrowing from your local library

More than 11,000 libraries in the United States lend Kindle versions of books through a system called Overdrive, which allows you to easily download books to your Fire tablet. The length of time for which you can borrow a book varies by library, and each library may have a slightly different system for borrowing books. You typically initiate the library loan from the library's website, enter your Amazon account information, and then specify the device you want to deliver the book to.

Here are the typical steps for borrowing Kindle books, but you should ask your library for the specific steps that work with its system:

1. Go to your library's website and search for ebooks.

   Note that you'll need a library card and PIN to borrow books.

2. Click the title you want to check out and then enter your library card information and PIN.

3. After you check out a title, choose the Get for Kindle option.

   You may then have to enter your Amazon.com account information to borrow the title.

4. Choose the title and your Fire tablet as the device you want the book delivered to; then choose Get Library Book to download the title.

Reading Books

After you get your hands on a Kindle book, you can begin to read by using the simple ereader tools in the Kindle ereader app. You may have used this app on another device, such as your computer, smartphone, or other tablet, though each version of this app has slightly different features. In the following sections, I go over the basics of how the Kindle ereader app works on Fire tablets.

You can get to the Home screen from anywhere in the ereader app. If a Home button isn't visible, just tap the page to display the Options bar, which includes a Home button. You'll also see settings for the book such as View (to change display settings) and Share (to share selected content via email, Facebook, or Twitter).

Going to the Fire library

When you tap Books on your Fire tablet screen, you open the Books library, containing downloaded content on the Device tab and content stored in the Cloud on the Cloud tab (see Figure 8-3). The active tab is the one displaying an orange underline. There's also a Store button that you use to go to the Amazon Bookstore to shop for books.

Figure 8-3: The Books library displays all your book purchases, and books stored in the Cloud on two tabs.

There are also several features in your Books library that you can use to get different perspectives on its contents and books that are popular with your friends:

✔ **Goodreads:** Tap the Goodreads button at the top of the screen to create a Goodreads account using your Facebook sign-in information. You can then display books that your friends are reading and their rating, if any, of the books or follow your favorite authors.

✔ **Sort titles:** Use the drop-down list under the Books library title to select By Author, By Recent, and By Title to view books by any of these three criteria (see Figure 8-4).

✔ **Identify new titles:** If you've just downloaded but haven't started reading a book, there will be a blue banner in the corner of the thumbnail with the word New on it (see Figure 8-5).

Figure 8-4: Sorting options in the Books library.

New books have a banner

Figure 8-5: New titles are easily identifiable.

Tap the Search button on the Options bar to search your Books library contents by title or author.

Opening a book

Remember the pleasure you took as a child in opening up a new book, awaiting the adventures or knowledge it had to impart! Opening your first ebook is likely to bring you a similar sort of pleasure because you access your book instantly and the tech interface is so much fun to play with.

To open a book from the Home screen, follow these steps:

1. **Tap Books.**

   The Books library opens.

2. **Locate the book you want to read (swipe upward if you need to reveal more books in the list).**

3. **Tap a book.**

   The book opens. If the book hasn't been downloaded to your Fire tablet, it begins downloading and takes only seconds to complete. Once download is complete, tap the book to open it.

If you never started to read the book, it opens on its title page. If you've read part of the book, it opens automatically to the last page you read. This last-read page is bookmarked in the Cloud by Amazon when you stop reading, so no matter what device you use to read it — your Fire tablet, computer, or smartphone, for example — you go to the last-read page immediately. You may see a prompt asking if you want to sync to the furthest read page among your devices.

You can also open a publication from Favorites or the Carousel. Read more about these features in Chapter 2.

Navigating a book

An open book just begs to be read. You're used to flipping pages in a physical book, but an ereader provides you with several ways to move around.

The simplest way to move one page forward or one page back is to tap or swipe your finger anywhere on the right side of the screen to move forward or the left side to move backward. Try this out by tapping on the right side to move from the title page to a page of text within the book.

With a book page displayed, tap the screen to see these buttons in the Options bar along the bottom of the screen (see Figure 8-6):

- **Home:** This button takes you to the Home screen.

- **Back:** Tap the button of a left-pointing arrow to go back one screen (not page).

- **Search:** Use the magnifying glass button found in the middle of the screen to initiate a search for text in the book.

Progress bar

Figure 8-6: A typical page of a book in the Kindle ereader app.

Just above the Options bar you'll see information about where you are in the book (both page number and percent of the total content read) and the Timeline, which you can use to move within the book; drag the white circle to the left (backward) or right (forward).

The Options bar buttons and the Play button for using Text-to-Speech are on the bottom of the screen. Plus, these tools are along the top of the screen:

✓ **View:** Use this button to access settings for font, background, and text spacing.

- ✔ **X-Ray:** Tap this button to view additional information about the book if it's available for that title.
- ✔ **Notes:** Displays any notes you have made in the book.
- ✔ **Goodreads:** Use this button to share your thoughts about the book via Twitter or Facebook.
- ✔ **Bookmarks:** Places a bookmark on the page.

You can also tap the Left Nav button, the button to the left of this set of tools, which contains options you can tap to

- ✔ Go to a particular page or location in the book.
- ✔ Sync to the last page you read on any device.
- ✔ Add a professional narration of the book if it's available; choosing this option takes you to the Amazon Store where you can purchase the audio narration for the book.
- ✔ Jump to the book title page, table of contents, or individual chapters.
- ✔ View more information about Reading Group questions or the author in books that contain them.
- ✔ Tap Mentioned in This Book, if it's available, to get further information about people, books, movies, or other popular content mentioned in the book.

The Progress bar along the bottom of the screen (refer to Figure 8-6) indicates how far along in the publication you are at the moment. To move around the publication, you can press the circle on this bar and drag it in either direction.

Reading children's books

Many children's books with extensive illustrations use what Amazon refers to as a *fixed layout,* meaning that the pages are fixed representations of how the pages look in the print book. This means that you can't enlarge and reduce the size of everything on the page at one time, you can't change the font style, and you can't change orientation: Each book is set in either landscape or portrait orientation. To move from page to page, you can swipe from right to left on the right page to flip it over.

Keep in mind that children's books are usually set up with blocks of text that go along with illustrations; that's why you can't enlarge all the text on an entire page. Instead, you enlarge a single block of text. To do this, double-tap a block of text, and the text becomes larger. When you subsequently swipe the page, you move to the next block of text, which enlarges (the previous block of text goes back to normal size). When you've read the last block of text on the page (typically in a two-page spread), swiping takes you to the next page. Double-tap the currently enlarged text again to go back to normal text size and proceed through the book. See Chapter 5 for more about using your Fire tablet with kids and the FreeTime Unlimited service for kids' content.

Diving In with Immersion Reading

Immersion Reading lets you buy the narration from an audiobook to go along with a print book you own. When you do, you can play the professional narration from your book, and text is highlighted as each word is spoken. This so-called Immersion Reading approach is supposed to help reader retention and plunge you deep into the reading experience.

To use Immersion Reading, follow these steps:

1. **Go to** www.amazon.com.

   You can use your computer browser or the Silk browser from your Fire. These steps are based on using a computer without touchscreen.

2. **Click Shop by Department⇨Books & Audible⇨Whispersync for Voice.**

3. **Click the Search for Your Matches link.**

4. **Enter your Amazon account information.**

   The books you own that have the Immersion Reading feature are displayed.

5. **Click the Upgrade with Audio button for the title you want to purchase.**

You can also locate the book you want to buy in the list of bestsellers when you choose Audible Audiobooks & More in the Books & Audible section of the Shop by Department menu, and then follow these steps:

1. **Find a book you want to buy and then click Buy or Buy with 1-Click, depending on how your account is set up.**

2. **If you choose Buy, you are presented with a price button; click it.**

3. **On the page that appears, click to buy the Audible audiobook.**

To play the narration, whether you added it to a book you already own or whether you purchased the audiobook version, follow these steps:

1. **From the Fire Home screen, tap Audiobooks.**

2. **In your library, tap to open the Immersion Reading–enabled book.**

3. **In the screen that appears (see Figure 8-7), tap the screen to display tools.**

4. **Tap the Play button at the bottom of the screen.**

   Each word is highlighted as it's spoken.

5. **Tap the Pause button when you want to pause the audio playback.**

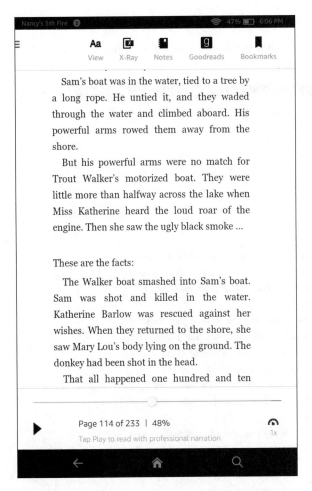

Figure 8-7: Play the narration of the audiobook from right within your Books library.

You can adjust the playback speed by tapping the Narration Speed button (in the bottom-right corner) and tapping it till you get to a playback speed you like.

X-Ray for Books

Although only some books are X-Ray—enabled at this point in time, if you find one that is, you can get information about characters and their back stories, as well as locations and other terms mentioned in the book.

Here's how to use X-Ray with books:

1. **Open a book that is X-Ray–enabled, like the one shown in Figure 8-8.**

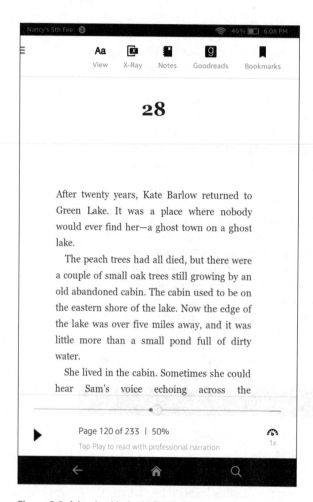

Figure 8-8: A book with the X-Ray button available.

2. **Tap the top of the screen to display the toolbar shown in the figure.**

   You see an X-Ray button.

3. **Tap the X-Ray button.**

   You see a list of items in the book.

4. **Tap to see Notable Clips, People, Terms, or Images.**

Note that these X-Ray categories may vary depending on the book (see Figure 8-9).

5. **Tap an item on the Timeline to go to different locations in the book where that item is mentioned.**

You can tap dots on the line above the first instance of the text to go to another occurrence or swipe to the right or left on the text to move to the next or previous instance.

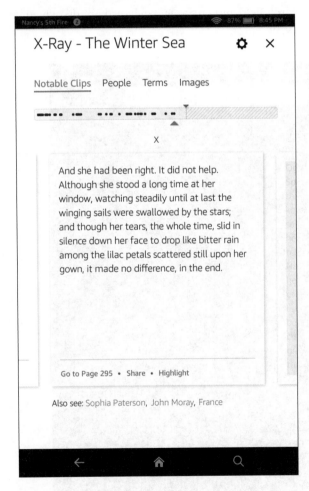

Figure 8-9: Get information about characters, terms, and images.

Searching in a book

Want to find that earlier reference to a character so that you can keep up with a plot? Or do you want to find any mention of Einstein in an e-encyclopedia? To find words or phrases in a book, you can use the Search feature.

Follow these steps to search a book:

1. **With a book open, tap the page to display the Options bar, if necessary.**
2. **Tap the Search button in the Options bar.**

   The Search field and onscreen keyboard are displayed, as shown in Figure 8-10.

Figure 8-10: Search for a word or phrase by using the Search field and onscreen keyboard.

3. **Enter a search term or phrase and then tap the Search key on the keyboard.**

   Search results are displayed, as shown in Figure 8-11.

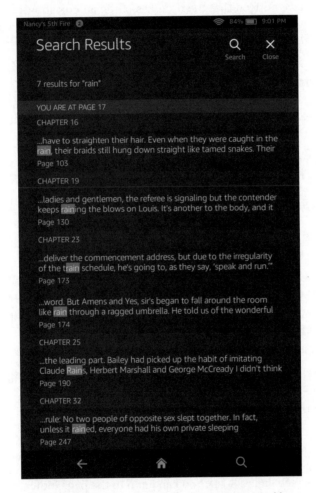

Figure 8-11: Search results indicate the search term with a highlight.

If you'd rather search the web, do this:

1. **Press a word or phrase to highlight it.**

   A dialog box opens.

2. **Tap the More button. (Look for three vertical dots.)**

3. **Tap Search the Web.**

   The Search the Web option takes you to search results for the term in the Bing search engine.

You may have noticed that the progress bar in a book shows both a page number (for example, page 24 out of a total of 178 pages) and a percentage. The percentage tells you how far you've progressed through the pages.

Bookmarking a page and highlighting text

If you find that perfect quote or a phrase that you just have to read again at a later time, you can use the Bookmark feature in Kindle ereader.

To place a bookmark on a page, display the page and tap near the top edge of the right corner of the page. A small bookmark ribbon appears on the page (see Figure 8-12). Tap the ribbon to remove it.

To highlight text:

1. **Press and hold your finger on the text.**

   Handles appear below the text on either side.

2. **If you want to select additional adjacent text to be highlighted, press your finger on one of these handles and drag to the left or right.**

3. **When the entire phrase or paragraph you want to highlight is selected, remove your finger.**

   A toolbar appears (see Figure 8-13).

4. **Tap the Color button and then tap one of the colored highlight boxes that appears.**

   The text is highlighted using the selected color.

When you place a bookmark on a page or highlight text within a book, you can then display a list of bookmarks and highlights by tapping the page and then tapping the Notes button at the top of the page to display your notes and marks (see Figure 8-14). You can jump to the page indicated by a bookmark or to highlighted text by tapping an item in this list.

When you press text and see the toolbar shown in Figure 8-13, a brief definition appears from the preinstalled *New Oxford American Dictionary*. In the definition window (you may have to scroll to the right to find it because Wikipedia and Translation and X-Ray windows may also appear), tap Full Definition to go to the full *Oxford Dictionary* definition. Tap the page and then tap the Back button to return to the book. See Chapter 10 for more about Fire's built-in dictionary.

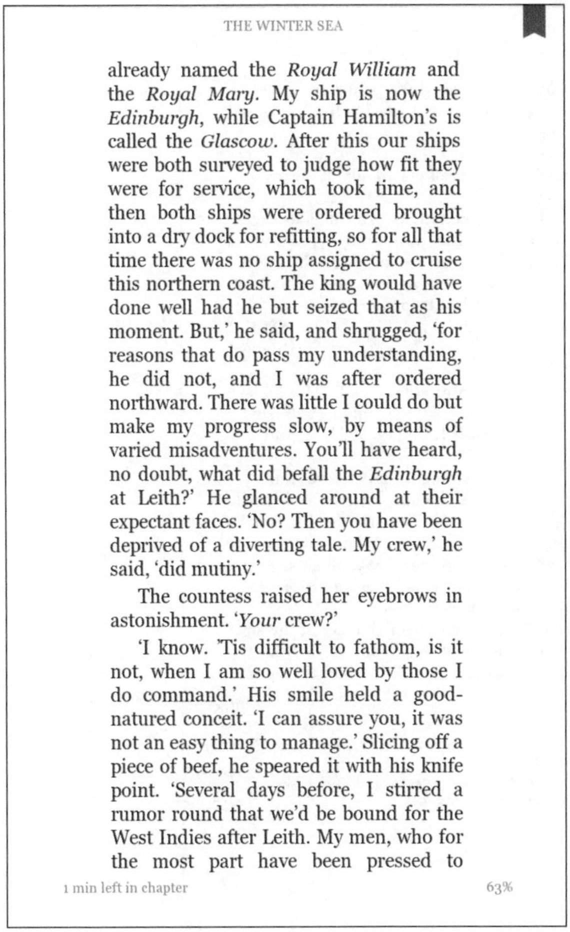

THE WINTER SEA

already named the *Royal William* and the *Royal Mary.* My ship is now the *Edinburgh*, while Captain Hamilton's is called the *Glascow.* After this our ships were both surveyed to judge how fit they were for service, which took time, and then both ships were ordered brought into a dry dock for refitting, so for all that time there was no ship assigned to cruise this northern coast. The king would have done well had he but seized that as his moment. But,' he said, and shrugged, 'for reasons that do pass my understanding, he did not, and I was after ordered northward. There was little I could do but make my progress slow, by means of varied misadventures. You'll have heard, no doubt, what did befall the *Edinburgh* at Leith?' He glanced around at their expectant faces. 'No? Then you have been deprived of a diverting tale. My crew,' he said, 'did mutiny.'

The countess raised her eyebrows in astonishment. '*Your* crew?'

'I know. 'Tis difficult to fathom, is it not, when I am so well loved by those I do command.' His smile held a good-natured conceit. 'I can assure you, it was not an easy thing to manage.' Slicing off a piece of beef, he speared it with his knife point. 'Several days before, I stirred a rumor round that we'd be bound for the West Indies after Leith. My men, who for the most part have been pressed to

1 min left in chapter   63%

Figure 8-12: A bookmarked page.

Modifying the appearance of a page

There are several things you can do to control how things appear on a page in Kindle ereader. First, you can make text larger or smaller and change the font. Second, you can choose a white, black, or sepia-toned background for a page. Finally, you can adjust the width of margins and spacing between lines.

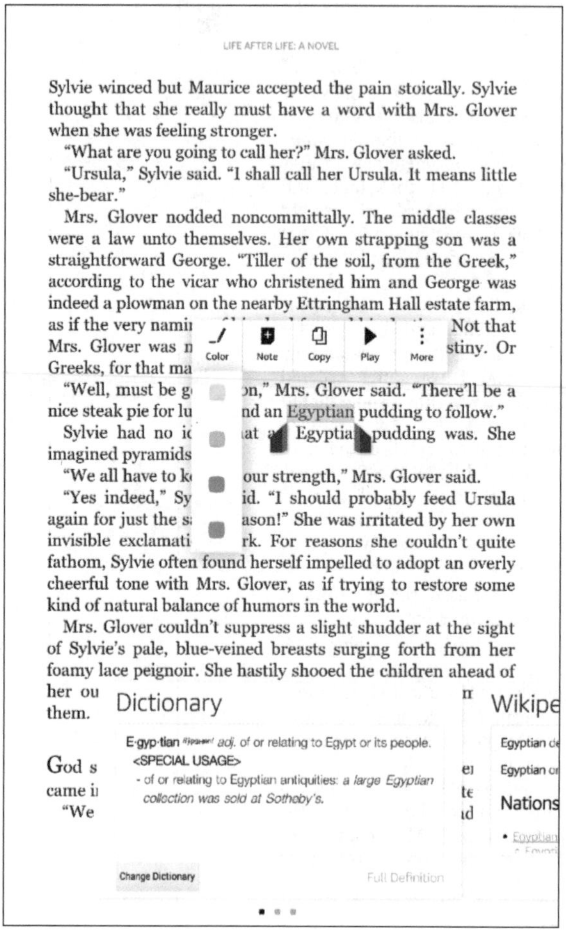

Figure 8-13: Press and drag either handle to enlarge the area of selected text.

To control all these settings, tap the page to display the tools along the top, and then tap the View button (the one with a capital and lowercase A). The options shown in Figure 8-15 appear:

- ✔ **Font Size:** Tap a particular font sample to change the size. Tap the down arrow to decrease the size and the up arrow to increase it.

- ✔ **Color Mode:** Tap a setting to display a different color for the page background. A white background gives you black text on a white page.

A black background gives you white text on a black page. A sepia background gives you a pale tan background and black text, and the green background may make reading easier on your eyes.

✔ **Margins:** Choose the margin setting you prefer.

✔ **Line Spacing:** Tap to select more or less space between lines.

✔ **Font:** Select a different font for the page.

✔ **Brightness:** Use the slider to make the page brighter or dimmer.

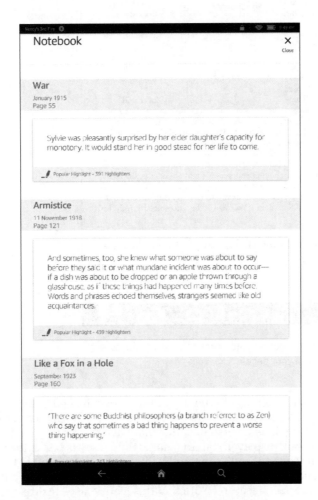

Figure 8-14: Both highlights and bookmarks are listed.

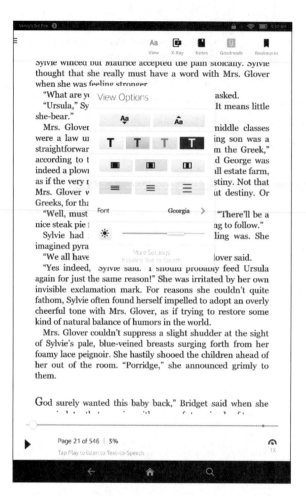

Figure 8-15: Settings options offer you some control over the appearance of your pages.

If you tap More Settings in the dialog box shown in Figure 8-15, the Text-to-Speech setting is available. This setting allows you turn on a feature that reads text to you in English for titles that have this feature enabled. With an enabled ebook displayed, tap to display the Progress bar at the bottom and tools along the top, and then tap the Play button to the left of the Progress bar. The audio begins. Tap the screen and then tap the Pause button to stop the Text-to-Speech feature. Note that this feature uses text-to-speech soft-ware. The somewhat mechanical voice is nowhere near as appealing as the professional actors who record audiobooks.

TIP

You can adjust brightness manually or have your Fire tablet do it automatically. Go to the Home screen and swipe down from the top of the screen to reveal the Quick Settings bar; then tap the Brightness button. If you press the white bar on the slider and move it to the left or right, you adjust brightness.

Sharing with others through Facebook or Twitter

When you're reading a book, you can share your thoughts with others via Facebook or Twitter and let them know how you liked the book. Follow these steps to share your thoughts on a book:

1. **With a book open, tap the screen to display the tools shown in Figure 8-16.**

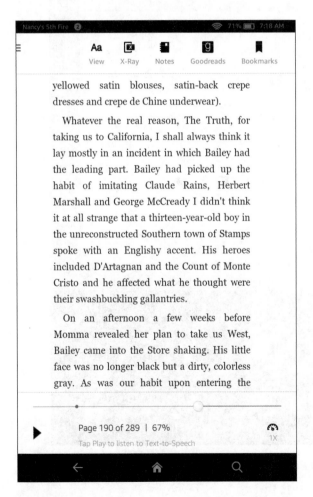

Figure 8-16: Ereader tools help you read and share your thoughts.

2. **Tap the Goodreads button near the top-right corner of the screen.**

3. **In the screen that appears (see Figure 8-17), you can tap to select an account to share with (Twitter or Facebook).**

   If asked, enter your email account and password to connect to the service. If you don't choose either account, you share only with your friends who also use Goodreads.

4. **Tap in the text field near the top of the page and then use the onscreen keyboard to enter a message.**

5. **Tap the Update button to share your thoughts on the book with others.**

Figure 8-17: Share your thoughts with the Kindle community.

Managing Publications

After you purchase content on Amazon, from apps to music and books, that content is archived in your Amazon Cloud library. You can organize your publications into collections.

If you finish reading a book on your Fire tablet, you can remove it from your device. The book is still in the Amazon Cloud, and you can re-download it to your Fire tablet at any time when you're connected to the Internet.

Creating collections

You can organize the content on your device by placing publications into collections (like folders). For example, you might have a collection of cookbooks, mysteries, or references.

To create a collection, do this:

1. **Go to your Books library and tap the Left Nav button.**

2. **Tap Collections.**

   A list of existing collections appears, if you have any.

3. **Tap the Add button and then enter a name for the collection.**

4. **Tap Next, tap to check any titles you want to add to the collection, and then tap Add.**

To view collections you've created and their contents, tap the Left Nav button in the Books library and then tap Collections. Tap a collection to view its contents.

Removing publications from your Fire tablet

To remove a book or magazine from your Fire libraries, follow these steps:

1. **On the Home screen, tap Books or Newsstand to display your library.**

2. **Locate and press your finger on the item you want to remove.**

   A menu appears (see Figure 8-18).

3. **Tap Remove. On the menu that appears, tap From Device.**

The thumbnail of the item remains in your Books library on the Cloud tab and on Favorites if you've placed it there, but it's gone from the On Device tab. To download and read the book again, just double-tap it in any of these locations, and the download begins.

Figure 8-18: Use this menu to remove a publication from your Fire tablet.

Unlike video and music, which you can stream from the Cloud without ever downloading them, books, magazines, and newspapers can't be read from the Cloud; they must be downloaded to a Kindle device before you can read them.

If you download a periodical and then press your finger on it in Newsstand, you see the Keep or Remove from Device options shown in Figure 8-18. At some point, old issues will be removed from your device unless you choose to keep them by using the Keep command.

Book samples will offer only a Delete option when you get to Step 3.

Buying and Reading Periodicals

Reading magazines and newspapers on your Fire is similar to reading books, with a few important differences. You navigate magazines a bit differently and can display them in two different views.

Follow these steps to buy and read a magazine or newspaper:

1. **From the Home screen, tap Newsstand.**

2. **Tap Store.**

3. **Tap a periodical and then tap Subscribe Now or Buy Issue to buy it.**

4. **Return to Newsstand and tap a magazine or newspaper in the Newsstand to read it.**

   Alternatively, you can tap an item on the Carousel from the Home screen.

   If the publication hasn't been downloaded to the device, it begins to download now.

5. **Tap the screen to display the Options bar and tools. Tap the Browse button to display thumbnails of pages (see Figure 8-19).**

6. **Tap a page to display it, and then swipe or tap on the right or left to scroll through these pages.**

7. **Tap the Left Nav button to display the articles in the publications.**

8. **Tap an item in the list to go to that item.**

 As with books, in most publications you can double-tap to enlarge text on the page; double-tap again to reduce the size of the text. You can also pinch and unpinch the touchscreen to move between larger and smaller views of a page's contents.

Reading Docs on Fire Tablets

Reading documents on your Fire tablet is a much more straightforward proposition than reading ebooks (meaning that there are fewer things you can do to navigate around a document or format the appearance of text). You can get docs onto your Fire by emailing them as attachments to your Kindle email account, or by transferring them from another device after you've connected your Fire tablet using the USB cord. On your computer, for example, you can just find the document you want and drag it to your Docs folder.

Figure 8-19: Scroll through thumbnails of pages to find the one you want.

Tap the Docs library button on the top of the Home screen and then locate and tap a document; or tap a doc on the Carousel or Favorites to open it.

Swipe left or right to move from page to page or use the thumbnails that appear along the bottom of the screen in many publications to move to further locations in the document.

You can make notes and highlights in Office WPS docs, but you can't in PDF documents. You can read more about working with docs in Fire in Chapter 12.

9

Playing Music

Music surrounds us as we go through our days. Portable devices provide us with decent-quality sound systems for listening to everything from Lady Gaga to Mozart, everywhere from the subway to the jogging path.

The ability to tap into Amazon's tremendous Music store (with more than 20 million songs at the time of this writing) and access it from any device, including your Fire tablet, means that you can build up your ideal music library and take it with you wherever you go. You can also *sideload* (transfer) music from other sources into your Fire tablet by using the provided micro USB cable.

Also, the addition of Dolby Digital Plus, audio powered through dual-driver stereo speakers (except for the 6-inch Fire, which has mono speakers), provides one of the finest listening experiences in the world of tablets. This system even optimizes sound for what you're playing so that music sounds like music rather than movie dialog and vice versa.

Music played through your Fire tablet's speakers sounds great, and music you experience through headsets uses Dolby Atmos multidimensional sound in the 8.9-inch Fire tablet, which allows you to hear sounds from different directions, which is especially welcome when viewing movies. In this chapter, you read about getting music onto your Fire tablet (see Chapter 6 for more about shopping for music) and how to use the simple tools in the Music library to play your music and create playlists.

Exploring the Music Library

All your music is stored in the Music library (see Figure 9-1), which you display by tapping the Music button on your Fire tablet Home screen. Your Recently Played selections are displayed.

Figure 9-1: The Music library is your central music repository.

The library can be organized by Playlists, Artists (as shown in Figure 9-2), Albums, Songs, or Genres. Tap the Left Nav button and then tap any of these categories to display the associated content.

Explore the Cloud Collection feature to organize all your content into collections via Amazon Cloud. Fire tablets come with unlimited Cloud storage for photos you take with your Fire camera and any content purchased from Amazon. See Chapter 1 for more about this feature.

Tap a selection to play it. At the bottom of the screen, in the Options bar, is a back arrow; when you're playing a musical selection, tapping this moves you back to the library. Also in the Options bar is a Search icon to help you find pieces of music.

Figure 9-2: The Artists category shows available content by performer.

When you tap the Left Nav button in the Music library, you also see Store options such as Best Sellers and New Releases. Further down, you find three more options: Add Music to Library, Settings, and Help. Note that at the top of the Left Nav menu are selections for Prime Music and Prime Playlists. Tap these to get free music options if you have a Prime account.

Searching for Music

If you want to find a certain music selection in your library, you can use the Search feature. This feature allows you to search your libraries, the Amazon Store, or the web.

Music library settings

If you tap the Left Nav button while in the Music app and then tap Settings, you see two main settings:

✔ **Automatic Downloads:** This allows you to automatically download selections to your Fire tablet whenever you save them to the Amazon Cloud.

✔ **Clear Cache:** This clears any data that has been stored to speed up future music downloads.

It's best to leave the Streaming Bitrate setting that follows these settings set to Auto to let your Fire tablet control the balance of speed and quality when downloading content.

When in you're in the Music library, follow these steps to search for content:

1. **Tap the Search button on the Options bar and enter the title of a piece of music or an artist's name in the Search screen (see Figure 9-3).**

2. **Tap Go on the onscreen keyboard.**

   The Fire tablet displays results that match the search term(s).

3. **Tap a result in Music to display music items in your library, the Music store, or the Cloud.**

When you're displaying the Store, you can tap the Search button at the top of the screen to search the Store only, or tap the Search button on the Options bar to display a Shop Amazon section and My Stuff section containing all of your music in the Amazon Cloud library.

Importing Music to the Cloud

One way to add music to your Fire Music library is by buying it from the Amazon Music Store.

You can also transfer a musical selection or collection stored on your computer (the music you've bought through iTunes, for example) by using the Fire tablet's micro USB cable. (Read more about this process in Chapter 2.)

In addition, the Amazon Cloud allows you to upload music from your computer; after you upload music, it's available to you through your Fire Music library.

Figure 9-3: The Search screen.

 TIP

Any MP3s you've purchased online from Amazon are automatically stored in the Amazon Cloud. For items you've imported, the first 250 are stored in the Amazon Cloud for free.

Follow these steps to upload music from your computer to the Amazon Cloud:

1. **Go to** www.amazon.com/cloudplayer **on your PC or Mac.**

2. **Sign into your Amazon account.**

   The page shown in Figure 9-4 is displayed.

Figure 9-4: The Amazon Cloud Player is where all your Amazon-purchased music resides.

3. **Click the Import Your Music button.**

   If a dialog box prompts you to get the Amazon Music Importer, follow instructions to download and install it.

4. **In the Amazon Music Importer window (see Figure 9-5), click the Start Scan button.**

   If you'd rather locate the items to import yourself, click the Browse Manually button. The following screen lists the number of songs that were found.

Figure 9-5: Tap into all your music by using the Amazon Music Importer.

5. **Click Import All. (If you prefer certain pieces of music to import from the Amazon Cloud, click Select Music, locate the music you want, and then click Import Selected.)**

   The import begins. After you upload items to your Amazon Cloud library, they're available to your Fire tablet on the Cloud tab of the Music library (see Figure 9-6).

Figure 9-6: Music stored in the Amazon Cloud Player is listed in your Fire Music library.

Playing Music

After you've found some music available to play (which I explain how to do in the preceding sections), playing that music is an easy task, one that will make fine use of your experience with every other music player you've ever encountered.

Note that if you want to listen to music when you're away from an Internet connection, you can still listen to the music you've downloaded to your Fire. To download music, open the Music library, press a selection that's only stored on the Amazon Cloud. On the menu that appears, tap Download. To remove music from the device at a later time, choose Remove from Device from the same menu.

The 6-inch Fire tablets have their speakers on the back; speakers are along the bottom of other models. For the best listening experience, keep the speaker uncovered, and definitely remove any surrounding cover or case from the back side!

Opening and playing a song

First, you have to locate an item to play, and then you can use the playback toolbar to control the playback. Follow these steps to play music from your Music library:

1. **Tap the Music button on the Home screen.**

2. **Locate an item you want to play.**

3. **If you're viewing albums, tap to open an album or playlist to view the contents.**

4. **Tap to play the song.**

   If you tap the first song in a group of music selections, such as an album or playlist, Fire begins to play all selections, starting with the one you tapped.

5. **Use the controls shown in Figure 9-7 to control playback.**

Note: The two items to the left of the Volume button allow you to continuously repeat the selection (the button with the oval consisting of two lines with arrows) and shuffle selections in an album (the *X* formed of two lines with arrows).

Tap the back arrow on the Options bar to go back to the album or playlist the song belongs to, shown in Figure 9-8. To go back to the Now Playing screen for the song, tap the information bar for the song that appears along the bottom of the screen.

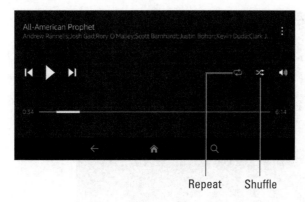

Repeat   Shuffle

Figure 9-7: Most of these tools are standard playback tools you've probably seen before.

Controlling sounds

With a tablet that's so media-centric, accessing music and video (plus games, with their accompanying screeches and beeps), it's important that you know how to control the volume.

When you're playing music, use the volume button on the right side of the playback controls to control sound. In addition, if you tap Display & Sounds in Settings, you see a volume slider that you can use to increase or decrease system volume. If you change the volume control in the playback tools in Music, you also adjust the system volume and vice versa.

X-Ray for Music

X-Ray displays information about artists when you're playing content such as movies; when you're playing Music, it even provides song lyrics. See Figure 9-9.

Not all music is X-Ray–enabled, but if you do own an enabled piece of music that you can identify by [+Lyrics] in the title, here's how X-Ray works:

1. **From the Home screen, tap Music.**

2. **Locate and tap a song to play it.**

3. **Tap the orange X-Ray Lyrics button shown in Figure 9-9.**

   The lyrics appear superimposed over the album image.

   If you hold your Fire in portrait orientation, you can tap X-Ray Lyrics again to expand the display of lyrics.

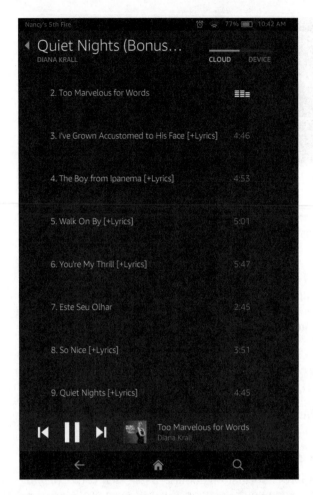

Figure 9-8: Tap the currently playing song title at the bottom of the screen to return to it.

Tap X-Ray Lyrics a third time to remove them from the screen. In either orientation you can tap an earlier or later lyric to move the recording to that spot in the song. See Figure 9-10.

4. **Tap the menu button (three vertical dots next to the song title) and then tap Go to Artist.**

   All songs from this artist are displayed.

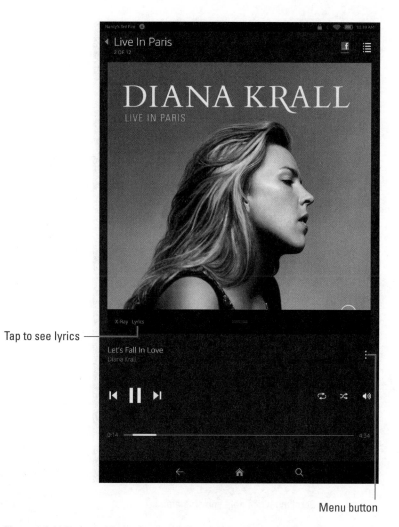

Tap to see lyrics

Menu button

Figure 9-9: X-Ray–enabled selections offer an X-Ray Lyrics option.

Creating playlists

Playlists allow you to create collections of songs that transcend the boundaries of albums or artists. For example, you might want to create a playlist of songs from a variety of sources for a romantic evening, a dance party, or a mellow road trip.

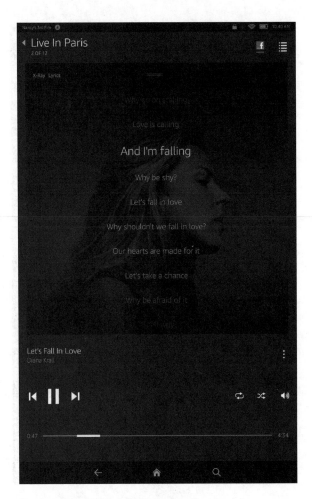

Figure 9-10: Scrolling lyrics help you sing along.

To create a playlist, follow these steps:

1. **Connect to a Wi-Fi network if you aren't already connected.**

   Creating a playlist requires a Wi-Fi connection because playlists are saved to the Cloud. If you have a 4G model Fire tablet, you can do this using your 4G connection.

2. **Tap Music on the Home screen and then tap the Left Nav button.**

3. **Tap Playlists and then tap the Add button (the one with a plus sign on it).**

   The Create New Playlist dialog box appears (see Figure 9-11).

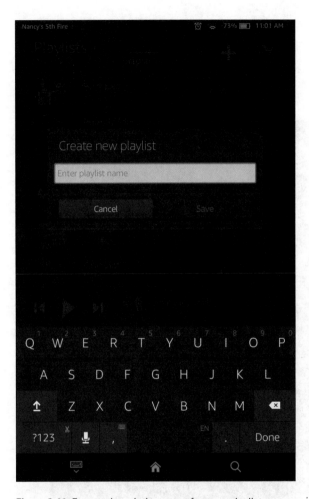

Figure 9-11: Enter a descriptive name for your playlist.

Getting sound out by cord or Bluetooth

If you want to use a set of headphones with your Fire tablet, which can improve the sound and remove extraneous noise, plug a compatible headphone into the headphone jack on the top of the device.

Alternatively, you can connect to a Bluetooth headset or speakers in close proximity. To enable Bluetooth, swipe down from the top of the screen to view Quick Settings, tap Wireless, and then tap Bluetooth. Tap the Bluetooth On button and then tap Pair a Bluetooth Device. In the dialog box that appears, nearby Bluetooth devices are displayed. If you move close to another device, tap the Scan button to scan again. Tap a device to establish a connection.

4. **Enter a name for your playlist.**

5. **Tap Save.**

   Your Fire tablet displays a screen containing a Search field and a list of songs stored on the device, as shown in Figure 9-12.

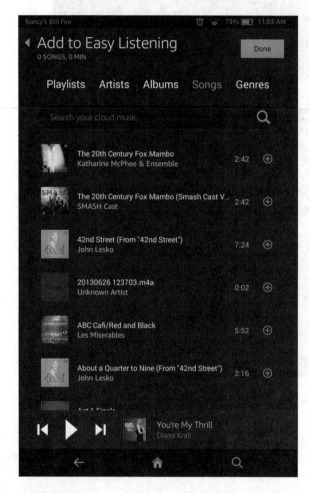

Figure 9-12: The items you buy and download can be stored in playlists.

6. **Tap the Add Song (+) button to the right of any song to select it.**

   If you've stored a lot of music and want to find a song without scrolling down the list, enter a song name in the Search field till the list narrows down to display it.

7. **Tap Done to save your playlist.**

   The Playlist is displayed (see Figure 9-13) and includes an Edit button that you can tap to edit the playlist contents.

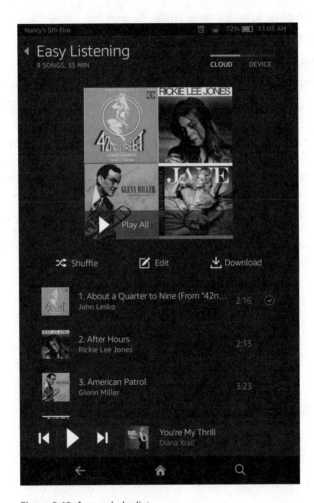

Figure 9-13: A saved playlist.

You can play the newly created playlist by simply tapping the Left Nav button and tapping Playlist. Tap the list you want to play and then tap Play All.

Editing a playlist

After you create a playlist, you can change the name of the list, add more songs, or delete some. To add songs to a playlist, follow these steps:

1. **Tap the Music app on the Home Screen.**

2. **Tap the Left Nav button and then tap Playlists.**

3. **Tap a playlist to display it.**

4. **Tap the Edit button.**

   Songs appear with a Delete (–) symbol next to them; tap this symbol to delete a song.

5. **Tap the Delete button to the right of any song to delete it from the playlist.**

6. **Tap the Add Songs button and then tap the Add button to the right of a song to add it to the playlist.**

7. **Tap Done to return to the playlist with the new songs added.**

If you want to rename the playlist, tap the Rename tab in Step 5, enter a new name in the dialog box that appears, and then tap Save.

10

Playing with Video and Cameras

In This Chapter

▶ Streaming or downloading videos

▶ Poring over your Videos library

▶ Watching movies and TV shows

▶ Getting the facts from X-Ray

▶ Using Second Screen and Display Mirroring

▶ Taking and managing photos

▶ Recording video with your Fire tablet

*P*laying video, both movies and TV shows, is a great use of your Fire tablet. The device has a bright, crisp screen, can easily be held in one hand, and is capable of streaming video from the Amazon Cloud, making for a typically seamless viewing experience without hogging memory on the tablet itself.

In addition, Amazon offers an amazing selection of video content, including absolutely free Prime Instant Videos (as long as you maintain a Prime account with Amazon beyond the free 30 days that come with the device).

You can discover the ins and outs of buying video content in Chapter 6. In this chapter, I explain how Amazon streams video content from the Cloud to your device, give you a look at the Fire tablet Videos library, and cover the steps involved in playing a video. In addition, I introduce you to the X-Ray for Video and Music feature that makes use of the Amazon-owned IMDb movie database to provide background info on many videos as you watch and provide an overview of the new Second Screen TV feature.

Finally, I discuss how you can use your Fire tablet to take and manage photos, and record videos of your own.

Streaming Versus Downloading

When you tap the Videos button on the Fire tablet Home screen, assuming you're connected to the Internet, you're immediately taken to the Amazon Instant Video Store (see Figure 10-1), rather than to a library of video titles.

(Most of the other buttons along the top, such as Music or Books, open to your library of content on the device or Cloud and offer a Store button to purchase new content. See Chapter 2 for more about working with libraries of content.)

Having Videos open the Video Store by default makes sense because, by design, Fire tablets are best used to stream videos from the Cloud rather than download them to your device. The device's relatively small memory (8, 16, 32, or 64GB, depending on the model you own) can't accommodate many video files, so instead, Amazon makes it easy for you to stream video content. If you do have some video content on your device, to go to your Videos library after you've opened the Videos app, tap the Left Nav button in the top-left corner and then tap Your Video Library.

Figure 10-1: The Amazon Video Store offers thousands of titles.

Swipe upward to scroll through the video content in the Instant Video store and view categories, including New Release Movies or TV shows (see Figure 10-2). In the store there are thousands of titles for free if you have an Amazon Prime account. (If you don't already have an Amazon Prime account, you get one free month of Amazon Prime with your purchase of a Fire tablet, after which you can purchase a membership for $99 a year.) You can also purchase or rent other video programs and stream them from the Cloud.

In the Video Store or library, you can tap the Left Nav button to display a list of categories of video content such as First Episode Free and For the Kids.

Figure 10-2: Browse thousands of free Prime titles in the Instant Video store.

Amazon's Whispersync technology keeps track of the spot in a video where you stopped watching on any device. You can later resume watching that video at that exact location on the Fire tablet, a PC, or Mac using the Amazon site, or one of more than 300 compatible TVs, Blu-ray Disc players, or other devices.

You *can* download videos you purchase (you can't download free Prime Instant Videos, however), which is useful if you want to watch them away from a Wi-Fi connection. Amazon is the only online streaming video company to offer this feature. It's a good idea to remove them from the device when you're back in range of Wi-Fi, to save space.

To delete a movie from your device:

1. **Tap Videos and then tap the Left Nav button and Your Video Library to open your content library.**

2. **Tap the Device tab.**

   Either the Movies or TV video content displays, depending on which tab you have selected.

3. **Press and hold your finger on the video you want to delete.**

4. **Tap Delete Download in the menu that appears.**

To delete a TV show from your device works a bit differently and takes a few more steps. (Who knows why?) From your Video Library:

1. **Tap the TV tab and then tap the Device tab.**

2. **Tap a TV show.**

3. **Tap just below the check mark to the right of the downloaded episode.**

4. **Tap Download Options.**

5. **Tap Delete Download.**

Looking at Your Videos Library

I'm betting that a lot of you are going to find that viewing video one-on-one on your Fire tablet is a great way to get your entertainment. The Fire tablet Videos library may become your favorite destination for buying, viewing, and organizing your video content.

To open the Amazon Instant Video Store, tap Videos on your Fire tablet Home screen (refer to Figure 10-1).

The store shows several video categories in rows running down the screen, such as Because You Watched, Recently Added, Top Movies, Top TV, or First Episode Free, as well as Your Watchlist. (I tell you more about Watchlist in a bit.)

Navigating categories

When you see a category that you want to explore, tap the words See More to the right of the category name (refer to Figure 10-2), and that category's contents are displayed.

For example, from the Video Store home page, follow these steps:

1. **Tap See More for the Top Movies on Prime Instant Video category.**

   A screen appears, with a down arrow next to the words "Top Movies, Prime" near the top left of the screen.

2. **Tap the down arrow to open a drop-down list.**

   Related categories such as Editor's Picks, For the Kids, Genres, and more appear in the list (see Figure 10-3). When you tap any of these categories, additional items related to that category appear to help you narrow down your search for content.

The categories may change over time, but the basic process of locating a selection and displaying its details should stay the same.

Creating your Watchlist

Watchlist is a way to make note of items you may want to watch in the future. When you add videos to your watchlist, you'll find them in two categories: Movies and TV. Here's how to add any video to your Watchlist:

1. **In the Amazon Video Store, tap and hold a video.**

   A menu appears.

2. **Tap Add to Watchlist.**

Tap any video in the various lists to get more details about it.

Searching for and filtering content

When you tap the Search button in the store, the Fire tablet keyboard pops up, and you can enter search criteria such as an actor's name or TV show name. Tap the Search key on the keyboard to display results.

Tap the Left Nav button and then tap Your Video Library to go to your Video library (see Figure 10-4). The library sports two tabs listing the following:

- All your videos stored in the Cloud
- Videos you've purchased that you have downloaded to the device

Figure 10-3: See what Amazon editors choose as their favorite videos in the Video store.

The tab that's orange is the active tab.

In addition to the Cloud and Device tabs, there are two buttons for filtering content: by Movies or TV programs. You can tap the Search button in the Options bar (on the right side of the screen when the Fire tablet is in land-scape orientation and at the bottom of the screen in portrait orientation) to search for a particular video.

Downloaded video content is listed chronologically by the date you down-loaded it.

Figure 10-4: The Fire tablet Videos library stored in the Amazon Cloud.

You can tap the Left Nav button and then tap For the Kids in any category to view videos appropriate for younger viewers.

Setting video quality

Tap the Left Nav button to display Settings and Help options for videos. (Keep swiping to get to the categories near the bottom.)

In Settings, you can choose settings for HD (high definition) and SD (standard definition and therefore lower quality than HD) download quality (see

Figure 10-5). If you set a quality preference, Fire won't ask you for your preference before downloading high-definition or standard-definition videos. Though it's a good idea to be selective about downloading HD videos because they can take up a lot of memory, you may grow tired of seeing the message every time you download your new favorite flick.

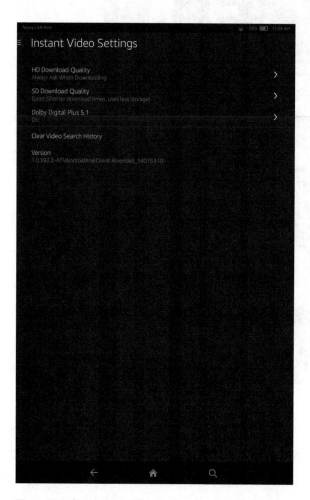

Figure 10-5: Check out options for downloading HD and SD videos here.

You can also tap and then turn on Dolby Digital Plus 5.1 in Settings to enhance your audio. Be careful about turning this on, though, as it takes up more of your Fire's memory and the bandwidth you need to stream video.

Opening and Playing a Video

Playing a video is a simple process. If the video has been downloaded to your device, open your library (tap Videos, tap the Left Nav button, and then tap Your Video Library), locate the video (using methods described in the preceding section), and then tap the video to play it. If you've played the video before, you may have to tap Resume or Start Over, or, if you've removed it from the device, press the Download button to get it going again (see Figure 10-6).

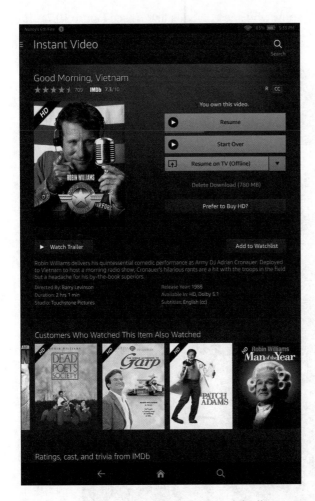

Figure 10-6: Start again or resume where you left off.

If you're streaming a video you've purchased that's stored in the Cloud, follow these steps:

1. **On the Fire tablet's Home screen, tap Videos.**

2. **Tap the Left Nav button in the top-left corner of the screen and then tap Your Video Library.**

3. **Tap the Cloud tab.**

   Videos you've rented (whose rental period hasn't expired) or purchased are displayed.

4. **Tap an item to open it.**

   If it's a TV show, you see episodes listed (see Figure 10-7). Tap one to open it or tap the Buy button to buy an entire season.

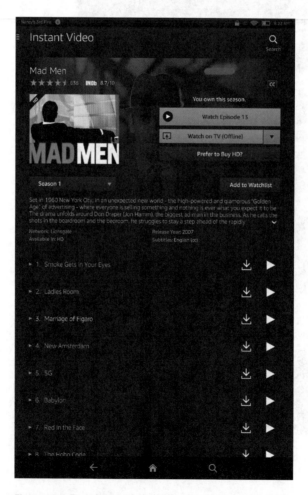

Figure 10-7: The episode list for a popular TV show.

5. **If it's a movie, at this point you see a description of the movie and the option of watching it or downloading it (see Figure 10-8).**

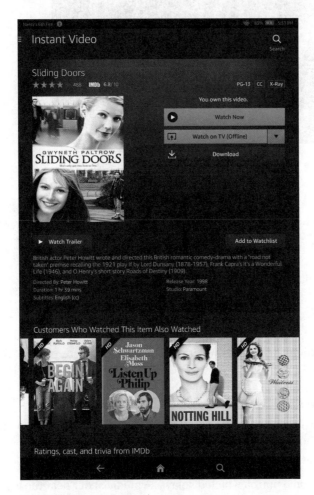

Figure 10-8: A new movie to watch!

6. **Tap the Watch Now button.**

   The playback controls appear.

7. **If you've already watched part of the video, tap the Resume button (see Figure 10-6).**

   If you'd rather see a video you've previously watched from its start, tap the Start Over button.

   The video appears full screen with playback controls along the bottom (see Figure 10-9).

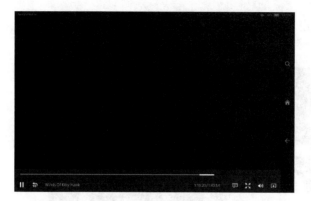

Figure 10-9: Move playback controls on a Fire tablet.

Note that the Fire tablet screen provides an extra-wide viewing angle. This means that you and those watching with you (well, maybe one person watching with you — it does have a 6-, 7-, 8.9-inch screen, after all) can see the content from the side as well as from straight on.

The familiar playback tools available here include

- ✔ Play.
- ✔ Pause.
- ✔ A progress bar and numerical indicator of where you are in the total time of the video.
- ✔ A button that shows a 10 and a backward arrow; tapping this button moves you ten seconds back in the video.
- ✔ A Captions button that opens a dialog box where you can turn closed-captioning on or off.
- ✔ A Full Screen button.
- ✔ A volume button which displays a volume slider near the top of the screen.
- ✔ A Watch On button which displays a menu to choose a compatible device to show the video on, such as a Smart TV.
- ✔ In the case of TV shows, a Next Episode button.

There's also a Back button in the Options bar that you can tap to stop playback and return to the movie description in the Instant Video store.

When you display a video's details in the Amazon Video Store, you can scroll down and read IMDb movie database trivia and information about the cast and reviews and ratings. See the later section, "Using X-Ray for Video and Movies," for more about this feature.

Using Second Screen and Display Mirroring

Second Screen is a Fire feature that enables you to "fling" movies and TV shows to your television. Second Screen streams the content to your TV and frees up your Fire tablet to use its other apps and features as you wish while watching the show. You can also use your Fire to control video playback and display X-Ray information about the movie or TV show you're watching.

Display Mirroring, on the other hand, is a method of having the display of a media-streaming device such as Amazon Fire TV or some Smart TVs match whatever is on your tablet screen. Using Display Mirroring, for example, you can have a game on your Fire screen and others in the room can view it on a TV as you control the game on your Fire. Display Mirroring only works with the 8.9-inch Fire tablet.

Several Samsung Smart TVs and some media streaming devices work with Second Screen. To use Second Screen, follow these steps:

1. **Open the Amazon Instant Video app on your TV.**
2. **Start playing the video on your Fire tablet.**
3. **Tap the Watch On button in the far-right corner of the bottom of your screen.**

   A dialog box appears, indicating that Fire is searching for compatible devices.

4. **Choose a display device that's connected to the same network as your Fire tablet.**

   Your video plays on your TV or other device.

To use Display Mirroring with a compatible device, follow these steps:

1. **Make sure you have set up your mirroring device to be available for screen mirroring using its settings.**
2. **Swipe down from the top of the Fire screen and tap Settings.**
3. **Tap Display & Sounds.**
4. **Tap Display Mirroring.**

   Fire looks for compatible devices.

5. **When Fire finds the device, tap it.**

   Whatever is shown on your Fire tablet appears on the other device's screen.

Using X-Ray for Video and Music

When the Fire tablet arrived, so did the X-Ray feature. X-Ray works with some books, music, and movies to give you access to facts about what you're reading, listening to, or watching. This feature is based in part on the IMDb database of movie trivia, which Amazon, coincidentally, owns. X-Ray continues to get more robust with each version of the Fire tablet, though at this point it works only with selected content. (If you want to try it, play an episode of *Downton Abbey*, free with your Prime Instant Video account.)

In the case of movies, when you're playing a video, the X-Ray feature provides information about the cast (see Figure 10-10), and if you tap a particular cast member, you get details about that person's career and other movies he or she has appeared in (Figure 10-11).

Figure 10-10: Find out more about the cast while watching the movie.

Figure 10-11: If you like the star, look for other movies featuring her here.

If you're playing music you bought from Amazon, with certain selections you can get both information about artists, such as what other artists they've worked with, and lyrics to some songs.

To display X-Ray information when playing a video, follow these steps:

1. **Tap the screen when an X-Ray–enabled movie or TV show is playing.**

   The cast list appears along the left of the screen.

2. **Tap the View All button to pause the playback and see the entire cast list as well as information about the director.**

3. **Tap a cast member.**

   Details like those shown in Figure 10-11 appear.

4. **Tap a tab above the cast list to view information about Characters, Trivia, Music, or Scenes.**

   To return to the video playback, tap the Back button on the Options bar.

Taking and Viewing Photos and Video

Fire tablet has a still and video camera built in so that you can take pictures and record videos. There's also a pre-installed Photos app for all you photography lovers. With improved features in Fire tablet, Photos allows you to view and do minor edits to photos.

Taking photos

All Fire tablet models have both a front-facing camera and a rear-facing camera (handy for those Skype calls when you want to show the other person what you're looking at).

You can use your front-facing camera on either model to take both still photos and videos using the Camera app. To take a photo, follow these steps:

1. **On the Home screen, scroll down to the Favorites grid and tap the Camera app.**

   The Camera opens.

2. **Tap the Front/Rear camera button for the direction you want to capture. (In portrait orientation, this appears on the top-left corner; in landscape, it's on the left side of the screen about halfway down.)**

   Typically you'd choose to shoot what you're looking at (rear facing) so you can use the tablet as a viewfinder.

3. **To set the app to take still photos, make sure the Camera symbol is the larger of the two icons on the button in the middle of the top row in portrait orientation, or the top of the left side in landscape; if it isn't, tap the button again (see Figure 10-12).**

4. **Hold the Fire and move it around until you see the image you want to capture.**

5. **Tap the Capture button (it's the circular one that looks like a little camera aperture).**

   Your picture is taken and appears as a thumbnail above the Capture button. You can tap the picture thumbnail to view it in your camera roll.

   Capture button

Figure 10-12: Set the Camera to still photos and then tap Capture to get your photo.

Recording video

Are your friend and you trying parasailing for the first time? Is it your daughter's 16th birthday? Do you want to capture midnight at your New Year's Eve party? You'll be happy to hear that you can use your Fire tablet to capture and play back video.

To capture a video, follow these steps:

1. **On the Home screen, swipe upward to scroll down to the Favorites grid and tap the Camera app.**

   The Camera opens.

2. **Tap the Camera/Video button. (In portrait orientation, this appears in the middle of the top of the screen; in landscape, it's on the top of the left side of the screen.)**

   To set this app to take videos, make sure that the video camera symbol is the larger of the two; if it isn't, tap the button again (refer to Figure 10-12).

4. **Tap the red Record button (see Figure 10-13).**

5. **When you're ready to stop recording video, tap the Stop button. (It replaced the Record button and looks like a small, white square in a red circle.)**

   Your video appears to the right of the Record button; tap it and then tap the Play button to play it.

Figure 10-13: Tap the big red button to begin recording.

Getting photos onto Fire tablet

When you first open the Photos app from the list of libraries and apps along the top of the Fire Home screen, you see photos you've taken organized by the date taken. Tap the Left Nav button and then tap Add Photos to add photos from other sources. A menu appears. Here you can choose to import photos from a Mobile Device, PC or Mac, Facebook, or to transfer them through a USB cable (see Figure 10-14).

Here's how these four options work:

✓ **Mobile Device.** Tap this option, enter your phone number, and tap Send. This sends a text to your phone with a link to get the Cloud Drive iPhone or Android app. Once you've downloaded and installed this app, your mobile phone photos will be uploaded to the Photo Library in the Amazon Cloud Drive and available to your Fire tablet.

✔ **PC or Mac.** Tap this, tap Email a Link to My Computer, and follow the instructions in the email you receive to upload photos from your PC or Mac to the Amazon Cloud Drive. After you do this, the photos are available in the Photos library on your Fire tablet.

✔ **Facebook.** Tap this and then tap Add Facebook Photos. On the following screen you give Amazon permission to access your Facebook account photos and upload them to the Cloud Drive, where you can, again, access them from your Fire tablet. This requires that you have installed and logged into the Facebook app on your tablet.

✔ **Transfer through USB.** Tap this, connect the USB cable that came with the Fire tablet to the Fire and to your computer, and then use File Explorer in Windows or the Finder on a Mac to copy photos to your tablet.

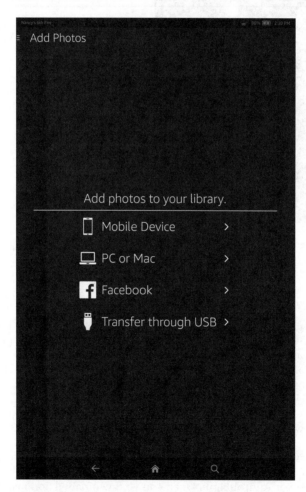

Figure 10-14: When you first open Photos, you are given an easy way to port content.

Viewing photos

After you load photos into your Pictures library, tap the Photos app listed alongside other libraries on the top of the Home screen. This app displays items in the Amazon Cloud Drive, and those on your device (see Figure 10-15) including photos or videos in your camera roll that have been taken with your Fire tablet and those that have been sideloaded to your Fire from a computer or other device. If you copy another folder of photos, it will come over as a separate album. Photos in albums are organized chronologically by the date you placed them on your Fire tablet. You can select what to view (Videos, Camera Roll, Cloud Drive, or Device) in the Left Nav menu.

Figure 10-15: Photo albums in the Gallery.

There are three main actions you can perform to view pictures:

- ✔ Tap an album to open it and view the pictures within it.
- ✔ Double-tap a picture to make it appear full screen.
- ✔ Swipe left or right to move through pictures in an album.

You can also tap the Share button that appears when you tap the screen while in Photos to share via email, Facebook, Skype, or Twitter, depending on what apps you've installed. In the email message that appears when you tap Email with the photo already attached, enter an address, subject, and a message (optional), and then tap the Send button.

To delete a photo, tap the Delete button that appears at the top of the screen when you tap the photo.

Note that when viewing photos on your Fire tablet, you can also enlarge or reduce a photo by pinching and unpinching with your fingers on the touchscreen.

Editing photos

When you have captured a photo, you can use editing tools to modify it. The set of editing tools available in the latest edition of the Photos app is impressive: You can do everything from cropping and reducing red-eye to rotating the photo, adjusting contrast and brightness, and even drawing or adding little stickers to a photo.

To edit a photo, follow these steps:

1. **On the Home screen, tap Photos in the libraries.**

2. **Locate a photo you want to edit and tap it.**

   If the photo is within an album, you may have to tap the album and then tap the photo you want to edit.

3. **Tap the screen to display tools and then tap Edit.**

   In the screen that appears (see Figure 10-16), use the tools at the bottom of the screen to edit the photo. You can scroll to the right to see additional tools.

4. **To try out some of these tools, tap the Rotate button and then tap the arrow buttons to rotate the image.**

5. **Tap the Back button on the Options bar to return to the main Edit screen.**

6. Tap the Stickers button and choose an image such as eyeglasses or a heart to place on your photo; when the sticker appears, press on it and drag it to the place on the photo where you want it to appear.

7. Tap the Back button on the Options bar to return to the main Edit screen.

8. Tap the Crop button and then press and drag the corners of the crop area in or out to include the portion of the photo you want to keep; tap Apply to crop the image.

9. To save your edits, tap the Done button.

Figure 10-16: The Photos app offers 18 different editing tools.

Editing tools are fun to explore; just open a photo and play around with all these amazing tools.

When you're displaying a photo full screen, tap the screen and in the tools that appear at the top of the screen, tap More. In the menu that appears you can use commands to create a slide show of the photos in the current album, print the photo, or upload the photo to the Cloud if it's only stored on your device; if the photo is only on the Cloud, the Download command is available to make photos stored in the Cloud available on your device.

Managing photos in the Amazon Cloud Drive

Amazon Cloud Drive offers 5GB of free storage, which will accommodate about 2,000 photos, though you get unlimited storage for all photos taken on an Amazon device. You can buy more storage for other content by spending anywhere from $10 to $500 a year for it.

Go to the Amazon Cloud Drive using a browser. (Go to Amazon.com, tap or click Your Account, and then tap or click Cloud Drive on the list that appears; you will have to tap Hello, Sign In to sign into your account at this point.) Double-tap the Pictures folder. Select an album or photo and then use the tools that appear at the bottom of the screen to download, share, or delete the photo.

11

Going Social

*F*ire tablets aren't just about reading books, watching movies, and playing music. There are several ways in which you can use the device to interact and communicate with others.

In this chapter, I help you explore how Fire tablets help you keep in touch with people using the pre-installed Contacts app. I also explain how Fire tablets integrate with Facebook and Twitter. Finally, I tell you all about using the Skype app and the new Fire tablet cameras and microphones to make video calls over the Internet.

Managing Contacts

The Contacts app pre-installed on Fire tablets is a basic but useful contact management tool. You can enter or import contact information, sort that information by several criteria, and use Contacts to address emails.

You can find Contacts by tapping its app on the Favorites grid at the bottom of the Home screen. Tap the Contacts app to display its main screen, as shown in Figure 11-1.

 Note that the Contacts screen differs slightly depending on whether you hold your tablet in portrait or landscape orientation. In Portrait there is no Search button in the top right of the screen, only Edit and New buttons; in Landscape the Search button, along with Edit and More. Tapping More reveals more commands, including New to create a new contact. Also, you see a preview of the selected contact's information on the right side of the screen providing his or her email address, phone number, and so on, and where the information came from (input on the device or imported, for example).

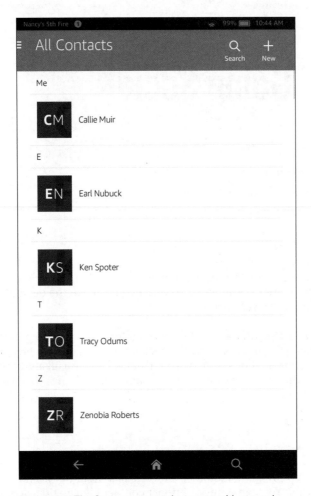

Figure 11-1: The Contacts app main screen with several contacts entered.

Importing contacts

If you have associated an email account with your Fire tablet, you can import all contacts from that account instead of entering each contact's information individually. (See Chapter 4 for more about setting up an email provider account to sync with your Fire tablet.)

After you have set up an associated email account (do this in Settings under Apps➪Email, Contacts, Calendar), Sync Contacts is on by default (see Figure 11-2) and your email account contacts are imported to your Fire tablet.

When you first open Contacts, your imported contacts will be listed there.

Note that you may see a message offering you the option to turn off the feature that backs your contacts up to the Cloud. Because contacts from your email account are saved to Amazon Cloud and then, therefore, available to your Fire tablet, you need to leave the feature turned to on to complete the import.

If you want to create a new account, you can tap the Add Account button in the Email, Contacts, Calendar screen of Settings. Enter another email address and tap Next. Enter a password and tap Next. Your Fire syncs with the account.

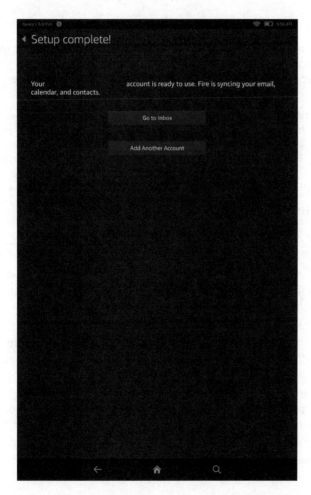

Figure 11-2: Sync to import contacts from your email account.

To sync your Facebook contacts with the Contact app in Fire tablets, go to Apps in Settings, tap Email, Contacts, Calendar, and then tap Contacts Settings. In the screen that appears, slide the Sync Facebook Contacts Off/On switch to On.

Creating new contacts

It's data entry time! Importing contacts (see the preceding section) is a nice shortcut, but you can also add contacts to your Amazon account or an email account you've set up on your Fire from the device itself.

To create a new contact, follow these steps:

1. **Tap the Contacts app on the Carousel or in the Apps library to open it, and then tap the New button in the upper-right corner. If you're in landscape orientation, tap More and then tap New in the menu that appears.**

   The first time you do this, you may see a dialog box that lists Amazon and any email accounts you've set up with an Add New Account button. After you've added an account, you'll see a New Contact screen (see Figure 11-3) that contains fields including First Name, Last Name, Phone, and so on. Tap the top field to select whether to add the contact to your Amazon Cloud account or an email account.

2. **Tap in a field such as First Name and enter text.**

   The onscreen keyboard appears when you tap in a field.

3. **When you're done entering text in one field, tap the Next button on the onscreen keyboard to go to the next field.**

   You have to scroll to the bottom if you want to enter detailed address information. You can tap Add More Fields at the bottom of the form to choose additional information fields to include.

4. **Tap Edit Image under the Photo icon at the top of the form and then tap Add Photo to add a photo.**

   Options appear for selecting photos, as shown in Figure 11-4. If you tap Take Photo, your Camera opens and you can take a photo that will be added to your Photos library. Closing the Camera brings you back to your new contact form where you can click the Edit Image menu again and choose Add Photo and proceed with these steps.

5. **Tap a photo to add it to the contact record.**

6. **Tap Save.**

   The contact information displays as shown in Figure 11-5.

Figure 11-3: The Contact form.

To edit the contact in portrait orientation, tap it in the Contacts list, and in the dialog box that appears, tap View Contact. If you're holding your Fire tablet in landscape orientation, tap the contact to select it and then tap the Edit button. To delete a contact, with the Contact open tap the More button and then tap Delete. To display all contacts, tap the Left Nav button from the Contacts main screen and then tap All Contacts.

Figure 11-4: Choose the Photo option.

Viewing and organizing contacts

You can use Settings to control how your contacts are organized and even save contacts to a list of VIPs in the Contacts app.

To sort your contacts, follow these steps:

1. **On the bar across the top of the Contacts list, tap the Left Nav button and then tap Settings.**

   The Email, Contacts, and Calendar settings appear.

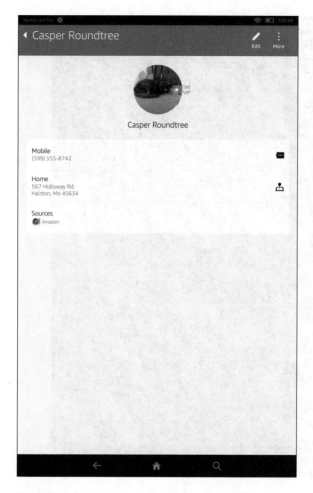

Figure 11-5: A contact record with photo included.

2. **Tap Contacts Settings.**

3. **Tap Sort Order of Contact Name to display the options shown in Figure 11-6.**

4. **Tap the associated setting to sort by first name or last name.**

You can also designate certain people as VIP, which adds a visual indicator of that status to the contact name. To make a contact a VIP, follow these steps:

1. **Tap Contacts in the Favorites grid on the Home screen.**

   The Contacts app opens.

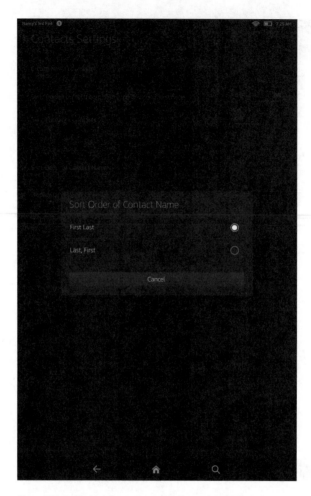

Figure 11-6: Choose from these basic sorting options.

2. **Tap the contact name you want to make a VIP.**

3. **Tap the star that appears next to the contact's name, as shown in Figure 11-7.**

   The star turns orange, indicating that this is a VIP.

4. **Scroll down your contacts.**

   You see a white star against an orange background at the top of the contact icon.

To view your VIP contacts only, locate the Contacts app on the Carousel and tap the star-shaped VIP button.

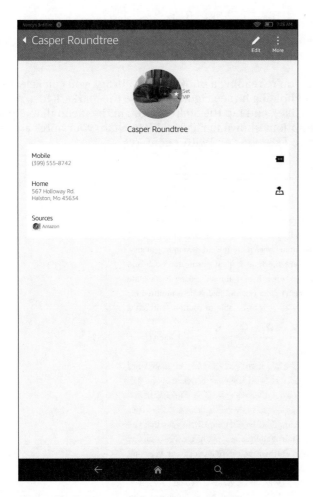

Figure 11-7: Tap the star to make someone a VIP.

You can also share contacts. With Contacts open, hold your tablet in landscape orientation, select a contact in the list, and then tap More⇨Share. (You can also just press and hold the contact name in the Contacts list and choose Share from the menu that appears.) In the email form that appears, enter a recipient(s) email address, enter a Subject and Message, and then tap Send.

Using Integrated Facebook and Twitter

If you want to work with your Facebook and Twitter accounts from your Fire tablet, you can download those free apps from the Amazon Appstore (and, in fact other social apps such as Tumblr and Vine). Once they're downloaded, open each app and log in.

In order to share items via Facebook and Twitter, you can use integrated tools in your Fire tablet itself. You can share photos, notes, and highlights from books, YouTube videos, contacts, and more.

For example, if you're reading a book in your library, you can select some text by pressing and holding it (see Figure 11-8; use the markers to expand the selection if you like), and tap the Share button in the menu that appears. This offers you the options shown in Figure 11-9 to share your notes and highlights via Goodreads to Facebook or Twitter contacts.

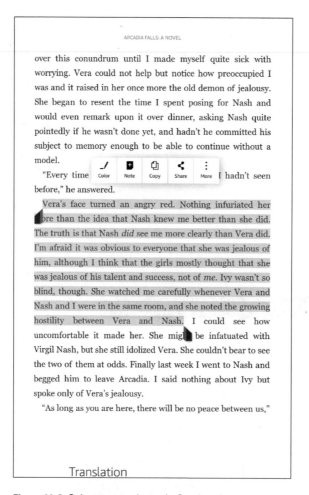

Figure 11-8: Select text to share via Goodreads.

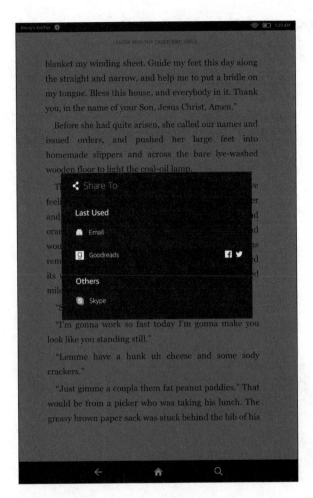

Figure 11-9: Share by signing into your Facebook or Twitter account.

To share via Facebook or Twitter, just tap one or both of those options (refer to Figure 11-9), and then tap Post. (See Chapter 8 for more about Goodreads.)

You can also share photos by displaying a photo in the Photos app and then tapping the Share button. Tap Email, Facebook, or Twitter and use the form that appears (see the email form in Figure 11-10) to enter a message or sign into your account to share the photo.

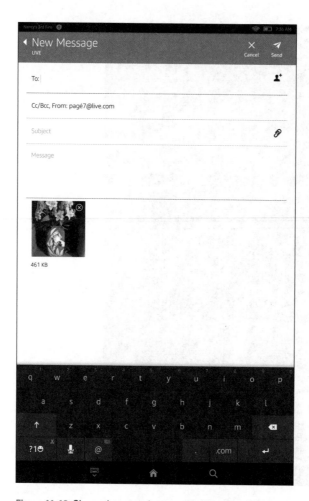

Figure 11-10: Share photos and more with friends on Facebook.

Making Calls with Skype

With Fire tablets come a camera (front facing and rear facing) and microphone. What they allow you to do is to make regular phone calls or video calls to others using the popular Skype app, for which you may already have an account. The Skype app for Fire tablets is free, but you will have to download it from the Amazon Appstore (see Chapter 6 for more about getting apps).

Conversations are given emphasis in Skype, with recent calls and chats front and center. Video call quality has been improved — which, together with the Fire tablet's crisp resolution, makes for some very clear HD (high definition) video indeed.

When you have downloaded the Skype app, tap Skype from the Favorites grid on the Home screen and then follow these steps:

1. **On the Welcome to Skype screen, you may be asked to tap Continue and then tap Accept on the following screen to accept terms and conditions.**

2. **Enter your Skype Name and password or Microsoft account User ID and password.**

   If you've never created a Skype account, tap the Create an Account button at this point and enter your name, Skype Name, password, email address, and phone number to create your Skype account.

3. **Tap the Sign In button and, on the following screen, tap Continue.**

   On the screen that appears (see Figure 11-11), you should tap the Echo/Sound Test button in the People section and then tap the Voice Call button (shaped like a phone handset) and record a message to verify that your connection is set up properly. Tap the Back button in the Options bar to return to the main Skype screen.

4. **At this point, you choose one of these options:**

   • **People:** This area displays a list of contacts you've saved to your Skype contacts. Tap one, and on the screen that appears, tap the Call button at the top (as shown in Figure 11-12) to place a call. Note that the Call button is near the bottom left instead of the top right of the screen in landscape orientation.

   • **Add:** Tap the Add button, the rightmost button of the three buttons near the top-left corner of the screen; then tap Add People or Add Number. Enter a name or number and the Skype app searches for a matching Skype user. When it returns information, tap a person, and then on the following screen, tap Add to Contacts. This provides you with an automated message telling the person that you want to add him or her to your Skype contacts. Tap Send to send the message. When the person responds positively, he or she is added to your Skype contacts.

   • **Call:** Tap the Call button, which is the leftmost button in the row of three buttons on the top of the Skype home screen, and then enter a phone number on the onscreen keypad that appears, as shown in Figure 11-13, and then tap the Call button.

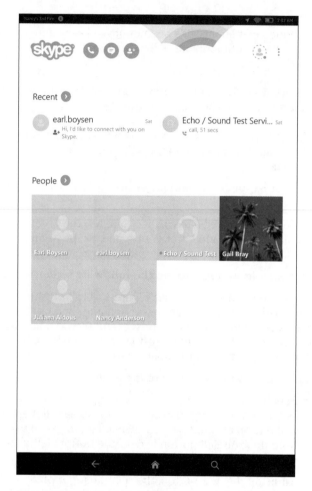

Figure 11-11: The main Skype screen offers a way to test your connection.

Here are a few more tips to remember about using Skype on your Fire tablets:

- You need to have credits to call people who aren't Skype users. Go to www.skype.com and sign in with your account information to buy credits.

- From the Skype main screen on Fire tablets, you can tap the Profile button on the right with a person's silhouette within a dotted-line circle and choose to be Available or Invisible to callers, add credits, or view your profile.

- You can tap an item in the Recent section of the Skype home screen to call someone you recently called again.

✔ Tap the Menu button and then tap the Settings option to access settings for receiving incoming calls, syncing contacts, signing in automatically, and so on, as shown in Figure 11-14.

Figure 11-12: Tap the Call button to place a call.

Figure 11-13: Enter any number here and place your call.

Figure 11-14: You can control your incoming and outgoing call experience with these settings.

12

Getting Productive

*F*ire tablets aren't just about watching movies and playing music. There are several ways in which you can use the devices to get your work done and share documents and images with others.

In this chapter, I help you explore how Fire tablets help you view and share documents. The new preinstalled Calendar app is useful for keeping on schedule, and it's covered in this chapter.

You can print documents and photos to a wireless printer. In addition, Office WPS is now integrated into every Fire tablet, allowing you to view, create, and edit Word, Excel, and PowerPoint documents. With improved cameras (front and rear), you can take both still photos and videos, and then manage your photos with the Photos app and Amazon Cloud.

And finally, I show you the easy-to-use features that make the free *New Oxford American Dictionary* a very useful tool for the writer in you.

Understanding Fire Docs

One of the items you see across the top of your Fire tablet Home screen is the Docs library (see Figure 12-1). Documents will be stored in the Docs library, to which this button provides access, and if you've viewed a document recently, it will also be available on the Carousel. You can also save docs to the Favorites grid on the bottom of the Home screen. (See Chapter 2 for more about Favorites.)

In the following sections, you discover how docs get onto your Fire tablet and how you can view and share them. I also provide some advice about using productivity software on Fire tablets to get your work done.

Figure 12-1: Tap the Docs button to open the Docs library.

Getting Docs onto Fire Tablets

Documents help you communicate information in forms ranging from newsletters to memos and slide shows. The ability to create, add, and edit documents on your Fire tablet makes it a very portable and useful tool.

Grabbing docs from your computer

To get a doc onto your Fire tablet, you can *sideload* (transfer) it from your PC or Mac by using the micro USB cable that comes with your Fire. Once connected, you can simply click and drag documents onto your tablet.

To sideload docs to your Fire tablet, grab the micro USB cable that came with the Fire and then follow these steps:

1. **Attach the micro USB end of the cable to your Fire tablet.**

2. **Disconnect the USB end of the cable from the power adapter and attach it to your computer.**

    Your Fire tablet will appear as a drive in Windows File Explorer or the Finder on a Mac (see Figure 12-2).

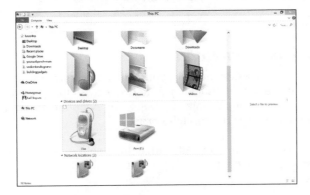

Figure 12-2: Options for opening up content of Fire tablets.

3. **Double-click the Fire drive icon, double-click Internal Storage item, and then click Documents to open and view files on the drive that appears (see Figure 12-3).**

Figure 12-3: Your Fire tablet appears like an external drive on your computer when attached using a micro USB cable.

4. **Click and drag files from your hard drive to the Documents folder.**

   You can also copy and paste documents from one drive to the other. Drag documents to the Documents folder, pictures to the Photos folder, audio files to the Music folder, and so on.

5. **Disconnect your Fire tablet from your computer.**

   You can now unplug the micro USB cord from your Fire tablet and computer.

Docs that you sideload are stored on your Fire tablet and in your Docs Cloud library.

Sending docs by email

You can also email a document to yourself at any email address, including your Fire email address. (Locate this address by swiping down to display Quick Settings and then tapping Settings⇨My Account. Your address appears under your name near the top-left corner.)

To email a document to yourself, with a document open, tap the Share button. A New Message form opens, ready for you to enter your email address, subject, and message.

Syncing with the Cloud

If you like, you can sync all your PC or Mac documents with your Amazon Cloud Drive and they will then be available on your Fire tablet. Here's the process to follow to sync documents:

1. **Tap Docs on the Home screen.**

   The Docs library appears (see Figure 12-4).

2. **Tap the Left Nav button.**

3. **Tap Add Docs to Your Library.**

4. **Tap Upload to Cloud Drive.**

5. **Tap Email Me a Link.**

6. **On your computer, open the email from Amazon in your email account; then click the Login to Cloud Drive link in the email and follow instructions to save the app on your computer.**

7. **When the download is complete, the download folder opens; right-click the Amazon Cloud Drive app and then click Open.**

8. **On the Cloud Drive Setup window that appears, click "Hello, Sign In."**

9. **Enter your email address and password and then click Sign in Using Our Secure Server.**

10. **On the following screen tap the Add Files button.**

    A window opens that you can drag files to.

11. **Drag a file into the window and then select a folder, such as Documents or Music, to place the file in.**

12. **Tap Add to Folder.**

13. **Drag files from your File Explorer or Finder folder on your computer into the Cloud Drive folder.**

    These files are now available to you on your Cloud Drive and in your Fire Docs library when you tap the Cloud tab.

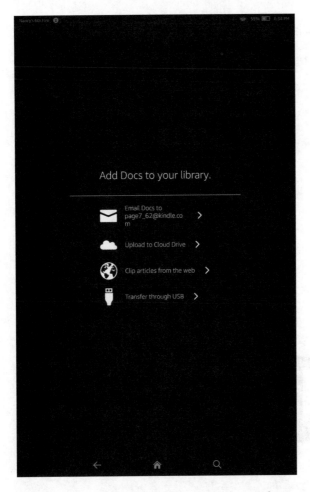

Figure 12-4: Use the Add Docs to Your Library buttons for information on how to get docs onto your Fire.

Understanding Document File Formats

Documents come in different formats. Some formats come from the originating software, such as Microsoft Word. Other formats can be opened by a variety of software programs, such as RTF documents that can be opened by any word processor program or PDF files. In Fire tablets, supported document formats include TXT, Microsoft Word DOCX (see Figure 12-5), HTML, RTF, and PDF (see Figure 12-6), as well as Amazon's Mobi and ASW formats. Some documents will be converted to one of these Amazon formats automatically.

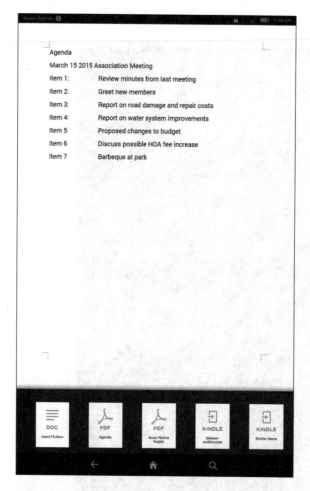

Figure 12-5: A Word document displayed on a Fire tablet.

You can also get a variety of common graphic file formats onto Fire tablets, and those graphic files will be stored in your Photos app. Amazon's Fire tablets even support compressed (Zip) file formats and automatically unzip them when they're transferred to your device via email.

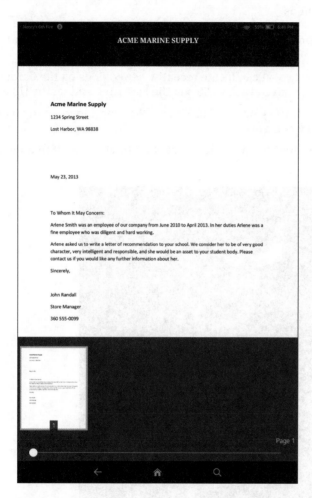

Figure 12-6: A PDF document displayed on a Fire tablet.

Working with Docs

Once you have a document on your Fire, you'll want to work with it, opening the doc, printing it, or emailing it to others. Those tasks are covered here.

Consider buying the new Fire Keyboard if you work on documents quite a bit. This accessory, with its touchpad, makes entering text on your tablet way easier. Get it from Amazon for $59.99.

Opening docs

After you put a doc onto your Fire tablet , you can view the document by following these steps:

1. **Tap the Docs button on the Fire tablet Home screen to open the Docs library.**

   Alternatively, you can locate recently viewed docs on the Carousel and docs you've saved to Favorites in the Favorites grid on the Home screen.

2. **When the library opens (see Figure 12-7), tap Cloud or Device to see the library contents**

3. **When you find the document you want to view, tap it to open it.**

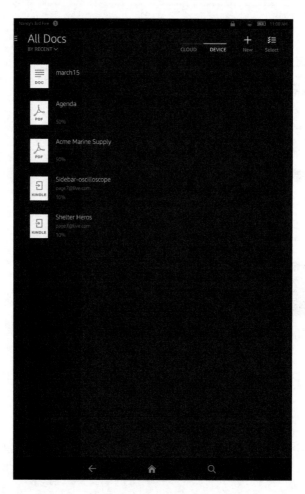

Figure 12-7: The Docs library with the Sort button at top left.

At this point in time, you can view documents and even edit ones that are compatible with Office WPS, including Word, Excel, and PowerPoint documents.

To search for a document, tap the Search button in the Options bar and type a document name or part of the name in the Search field. Tap a document listed in My Stuff to open it.

Emailing docs

When you have a doc on your Fire, you can view it as well as share it with others as an email attachment. Follow these steps to attach a doc to an email message:

1. **From the Home screen swipe upward to scroll down to the Favorites grid.**

   A list of favorite installed apps appears. If you've removed the Email app from your Favorites, look for it by tapping the Apps library.

2. **Tap the Email app.**

   The Email app opens.

3. **If necessary, tap your Inbox to display it and then tap the New button (see Figure 12-8).**

   A blank email form appears, as shown in Figure 12-9.

4. **Enter an email address in the To field, a subject, and a message.**

5. **Tap the paperclip-shaped Attach button on the right of the Subject line.**

   A menu appears (see Figure 12-10).

6. **Tap Attach a File.**

7. **Tap Office WPS.**

8. **Tap a folder and then tap the document you want to send.**

   You return to the email form with the document attached.

9. **Tap Send.**

   Your document goes on its way, attached to your email.

Note that people can send documents to you via email and they'll appear within the Docs library when you tap the emailed attachment and then tap Save. Tap the Email button near the top of that library to view your Fire email address.

Figure 12-8: Tap New to get going with composing an email.

Printing docs

If you have a compatible wireless printer from Epson, HP, Canon, Samsung, or Ricoh, you can print the following items from your Fire tablet:

- ✓ Documents including spreadsheets, word processor documents, and presentations
- ✓ Emails
- ✓ Contact details
- ✓ Events from your Calendar app
- ✓ Web pages from the Silk browser
- ✓ Photos

Figure 12-9: A blank form waiting for you to enter an email address, subject, and message.

You'll have to download a printer add-on program for your printer, called a *plug-in,* to make this work. Check the Fire User Guide for a list of links for these plug-ins. After you've downloaded this plug-in, simply locate an item to print and press on it on your Fire screen. Tap Print on the menu that appears. Tap your printer in the list of printers that appears, choose the number of copies, and then tap Print.

After you connect to your printer, you can tap More Options to access options for color, paper size, and page orientation.

Figure 12-10: Attaching a doc to an email message.

Working with WPS Office

If you want to do more than view documents on your Fire, consider using the integrated app called WPS Office (see Figure 12-11). This app gives you the ability to create, view, and edit word processor, spreadsheet, and presentation files. The popular Microsoft Office suite products Word, Excel, and PowerPoint are supported in this app.

WPS also supports files using the TXT format so you can view and edit files saved in that format from just about any word processing program.

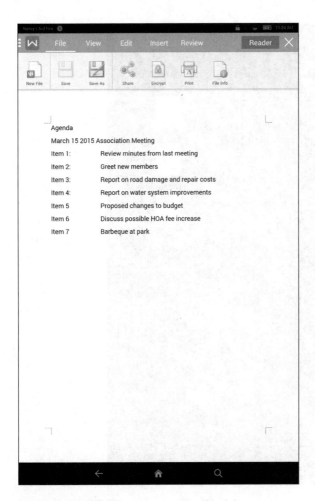

Figure 12-11: WPS Office open to edit a Word document.

Opening a document in WPS Office

You open new WPS Office documents from the Docs library.

To open a new, blank document, tap Docs and then tap the New button (represented by a + symbol). In the drop-down menu that appears (see Figure 12-12), tap any of the three document types: .doc for a Word document; .xls for Excel; and .ppt for PowerPoint.

To open an existing document, from the Docs library tap the one you want to open in the list of documents.

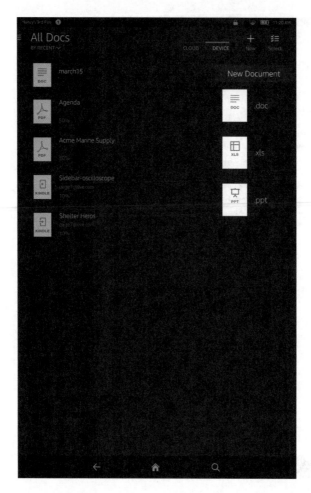

Figure 12-12: Pick the format associated with the type of document you want to create.

To sync the documents on your PC or Mac with Amazon Cloud Drive, click the Sync button in the Docs library and follow directions to install links to Cloud Drive. Any documents you place on that drive will appear in your Fire Docs library.

Using editing tools

Although the scope of this book doesn't allow for an in-depth tutorial on using all the formatting tools offered by the various apps supported by WPS Office, I can give you an overview.

When you have a document open in an app, there are several menus along the top. In a Word doc, for example, you have File, View, Edit, Insert, and Review.

Tap the Edit menu and a set of tools appears just below the row of menus (see Figure 12-13). These tools include Undo, Redo, Copy, Paste, Font, Paragraph, Bullets, Style, Page Background, and Page Setup. You have to scroll to the right to see all the buttons on this and many other toolbars. Note that the tools available in Excel and PowerPoint documents will vary from the tools in Word documents.

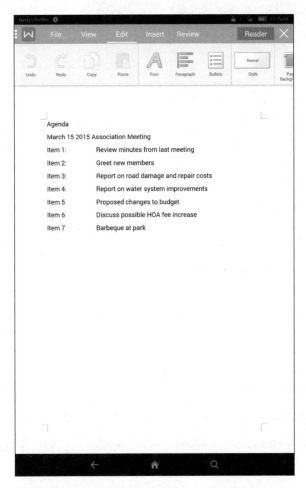

Figure 12-13: An assortment of pretty sophisticated editing tools is available to you in WPS Office.

Tap the Font button and you see a new set of tools for working with text. For example, you can set the font style, increase and decrease the size of text, use Bold, Italic, and Underline formatting, change text color, add a highlight, and more. Text-formatting tools are somewhat consistent in Word and PowerPoint documents.

To save a document, tap the File menu and then tap Save. Backspace over the default document name (typically Document (1), or the like) and give it a new name. Tap Save. You'll now find the document listed in the Docs library, where you can open it and modify it at any time.

Check out the Review menu in Word documents. This menu offers tools such as Spell Check, and the ability to track edits in the document in Revise mode, as well as tools for entering comments and an Ink menu for marking up the document using your finger on the Fire screen.

Staying on Time with Calendar

The pre-installed Calendar app offers a simple calendar interface, which you can display by day, week, or month, as well as in a List view. The Calendar app allows you to sync with calendars from your email account and then view and edit events and create new events.

Calendar settings and views

Before you can use many of Calendar's features, you might want to set up an email account for a service that contains a calendar feature. Your email calendar events will then automatically be synced with your Fire Calendar app. You can also enter and edit events right in the Calendar app on your Fire. That task is covered next.

You can see which calendars you're synced with at any time by tapping the Left Nav button while in the Calendar app. Tap one of these calendars to turn it off or on.

You can manage Calendar settings by opening the Calendar app on Fire. (You'll find it in your Favorites grid at the bottom of the Home screen.) Tap the Left Nav button and then tap Settings. Tap Calendar Settings on the following screen to modify features such as when the week starts, time zone, and more.

When you first open Calendar, which is also available in the Favorites grid, you see the blank calendar shown in Figure 12-14.

Tap the buttons along the bottom of the screen to display the calendar by Day, Week, or Month, or to display a List of events.

To move to other dates, swipe to the left or right. In Day view, these buttons will be dates just before and after the currently displayed day; in Week view, the buttons will be labeled for weeks just before and after the current week; and in Month view, you move to the previous or next month.

Figure 12-14: The Calendar app can be coordinated with your email account calendar.

 If you've set up a Facebook account on your Fire, you will see a Birthday Calendar in the Navigation menu. Tap this option to add birthdays from friends in your Facebook account, or tap U.S. Holidays to add a notation of the holidays to related dates.

Adding a new event

Besides getting events from your email calendar, you can also add individual events in your Calendar app. When you create an event in your Calendar app, it is copied to your email application's calendar.

Here are the steps to follow to add an event:

1. **From any view, tap the New button (refer to Figure 12-14).**

2. **In the screen shown in Figure 12-15, add the details of your event, such as title, location, start and end time, and so on.**

   If you want to have the event repeat (say, every Tuesday), tap the Repeat drop-down list and choose an interval; if you want a reminder in Notifications, tap Reminders and choose how far ahead of the event the reminder should appear.

3. **Tap Done to save the event.**

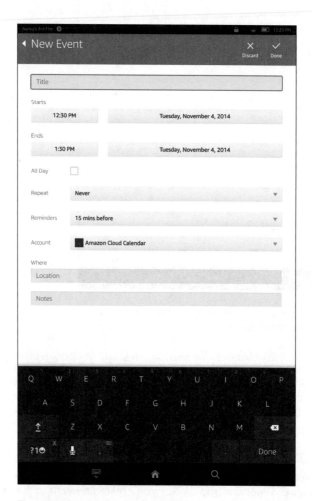

Figure 12-15: Add your event details.

If you'd like to invite others to the event, tap the Contacts button in the Guests field in the New event form; then tap to choose people from your Contacts list to invite. Each person you invite will receive an email about the event and the event will appear in his or her calendar.

To edit an event, simply tap to open it, tap the More button, and then tap Edit on the menu that appears.

Using the New Oxford American Dictionary

If you tap the Books button and tap the On Device tab, you'll see the *New Oxford American Dictionary* in your books library. Amazon thoughtfully provided this book to help you find your way with words.

In addition to being able to browse through the dictionary, when you press and hold most words in a book or magazine, a dictionary definition from the *New Oxford American Dictionary* is displayed (see Figure 12-16). You can tap the Full Definition button to go to the full dictionary entry.

When you open the dictionary, you can flick from page to page; entries are arranged here alphabetically, as with any dictionary.

As with any ebook, you can tap the View button at the top of the page to adjust font size, line spacing, margins, and the background color of the pages. You can also tap the Left Nav button and then tap Search to locate a specific word. You can tap the Left Nav button and sync to the last-read page (not so useful in a dictionary) or go to a specific page or location in the book (but this only uses a numerical location clear only to those at Amazon, so you might be better off dragging the progress bar to a later location or using the Search feature).

That's about all there is to the dictionary, but it can prove to be a handy resource for those who love words.

See Chapter 8 for more about reading all kinds of ebooks on a Fire.

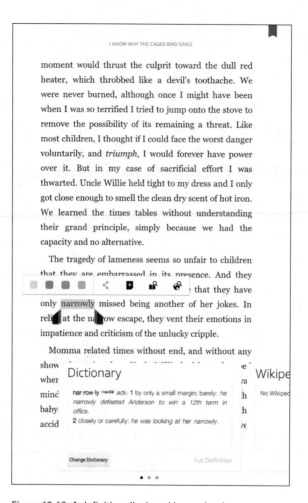

Figure 12-16: A definition displayed in an ebook.

Part IV
The Part of Tens

Visit www.dummies.com/extras/firetablets to read about ten great kid apps.

In this part . . .

- ✔ Get tips for how to get the most from your Fire tablet.
- ✔ Get introduced to some fun, helpful, or productive apps.

13

Ten Great Tips for Your Tablet

In This Chapter

▶ Customizing your Fire tablet's settings

▶ Accessing apps from sources other than Amazon

▶ Exploring the Clock app

▶ Getting rid of an app

▶ Managing storage

In this book I cover most of the major apps and features of Fire tablets to help beginners get up to speed with their devices. However, little tips and tricks can improve your Fire experience.

In this chapter I provide ten-plus tips and tricks that allow you to fine-tune Fire settings, keep your data safer, find apps beyond the Amazon Appstore, explore the Clock app's simple features, control data storage, and more. I encourage you to continue pushing the boundaries of what you can do with your Fire tablet.

Changing Your Fire Tablet's Name

You created a name for your Fire tablet when you set it up. When you get tired of a name like *Sally's Fifth Tablet,* or you want to give your tablet to your mother-in-law and feel that *Sexy Kitty* isn't quite right, how do you change your tablet's name?

Fortunately, it's easy to do. Just follow these simple steps to change your Fire's name:

1. **Swipe down from the top to reveal the Quick Settings bar.**

2. **Tap Settings.**

3. **Tap Device Options.**

4. **Tap Change Your Fire's Name.**

   The screen shown in Figure 13-1 appears.

5. **Tap at the right side of the current name and then press the Backspace key on the onscreen keyboard.**

6. **Type a new name on the keyboard.**

7. **Tap Save.**

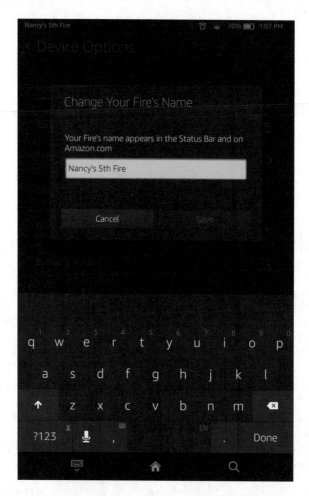

Figure 13-1: Give your Fire a new identity using this dialog box.

Removing Apps from the Carousel

The Carousel is the place where items you've recently opened, from books to apps and videos, appear. Although the operating system automatically places recently opened items there, you do have some control over what appears in the Carousel.

Follow these steps to remove an item from the Carousel:

1. **From the Home screen, scroll in the Carousel to display the item you want to remove.**

2. **Press the item until a menu appears at the top of the screen (see Figure 13-2).**

Figure 13-2: Remove items from the Carousel so you can find the items you need there more quickly.

3. **Tap Remove.**

   The item is removed. To add it to the Carousel again, just open it from the related app; your Fire adds it back to the Carousel again.

Performing a Hard Reset

Just like a computer, a tablet can crash and stop working now and then. When that happens with your Fire tablet, you can easily perform the equivalent of a reboot with your computer with a technique called a *hard reset*.

This one's simple. Press and hold the Power button on the top of the Fire tablet for about 20 seconds. (Ignore the Do You Want to Shut Down your Fire prompt and just wait for the device to turn off.) Press and hold the Power button again, and your Fire starts up, often causing whatever made it crash to resolve itself.

Encrypting Your Data

For most people, *encrypting* data (treating the data so it can't be read by others) isn't that important. On a Fire tablet your data consists of your documents, photos, and so on, and these usually aren't State secrets. For the most part, being able to encrypt data on tablets is the concern of administrators for organizations who want to protect data on tablets being used in the field.

Still, if you have data on your Fire that you want to keep private, you can use a setting to encrypt the data on the tablet. You should know that if you encrypt your data you'll be required to enter a password in addition to any lock screen password you may have set up to access your Fire tablet. In addition, encrypting your data requires that your Fire be at 80-percent charge or more, and be plugged in while encrypting. The process takes about an hour or more, and encryption will be disabled if you reset your Fire to factory settings.

If all that doesn't deter you, here's how you set up encryption after you make sure you have at least an 80-percent charge and your power cord is connected:

1. **Swipe down from the top of the Fire screen and tap Settings.**

2. **Tap Security & Privacy.**

3. **In the settings that appear, tap Encryption.**

   The screen shown in Figure 13-3 appears, offering the warnings I outline earlier.

4. **Tap Encrypt Tablet to proceed.**

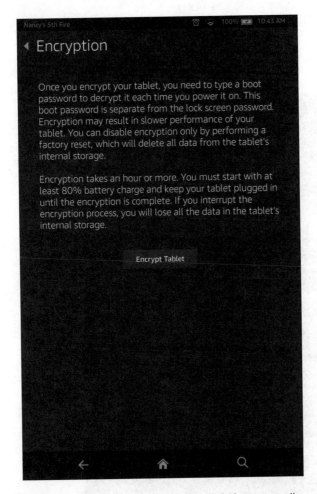

Figure 13-3: Read these warnings carefully before proceeding with encryption.

Accessing Apps from Other Sources

You can use a hidden setting that allows you to sideload apps you obtain from sources other than Amazon. When you *sideload,* you transfer to your Fire tablet from your computer. Follow these steps to change this setting:

1. **Swipe down on your Fire to reveal Quick Settings.**

2. **Tap Settings⇨Applications.**

3. **Tap the Off/On switch for the Apps from Unknown Sources setting.**

   The setting is turned on (see Figure 13-4). Now you can install apps that you got somewhere other than the Amazon Appstore on your Fire tablet.

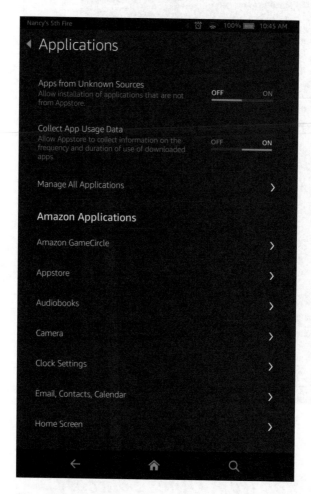

Figure 13-4: This obscure setting is what controls where you can get your apps.

Using the Clock App

The Clock app is preinstalled on your Fire tablet, and it's pretty simple to use. You'll find it in the Favorites grid (unless you've removed it, in which case you'll find it in the Apps library).

Tap the Clock app and you see the time and two settings: Weekdays and Weekends. If you tap to turn on Weekdays, for example, and then add an alarm, Monday through Friday will be selected for the alarm for you.

Follow these steps to set an alarm:

1. **Tap the New button (shaped like a plus sign).**
2. **On the screen that appears (see Figure 13-5), tap numbers to enter a time.**

Figure 13-5: Tap the numbers to enter your alarm time.

3. **Tap AM or PM.**

4. **Tap Repeat.**

5. **Tap the check box for the day of the week you want the alarm to occur.**

   For example, if you want an alarm at 7 a.m. every weekday, tap the Monday through Friday check boxes.

6. **Tap the Alarm Repeat back arrow to return to the Alarm screen.**

7. **If you want to change what sound plays for the alarm, tap Sound and then select a different sound.**

8. **Tap the Alarm Sound back arrow, and then tap Set Alarm to save your alarm settings.**

   The alarm now appears on your Clock screen; you can tap to edit it and use the switch on that screen to turn the alarm on and off.

By tapping the Left Nav button in the Clock app, you can add cities whose time you want to display, use Timer and Stopwatch features, and even display a Nightstand mode that displays only the time in a muted orange color that's readable in the dark.

Uninstalling or Force-Stopping an App

Some apps that run in the background can use up your memory resources on your tablet. To minimize the impact of apps using up your memory, you can force an app to stop running. In addition, if there's an app you'd rather get rid of, you can uninstall it.

To do either of these actions, follow these steps:

1. **Swipe down to display the Quick Settings bar and then tap Settings.**

2. **Tap Applications.**

3. **Tap Manage All Applications.**

4. **Tap an app.**

   Figure 13-6 shows the screen that appears when I select the Camera app.

5. **Tap the Force Stop button.**

   The app stops running.

6. **If you want to get rid of the app, tap the Uninstall button.**

   A confirmation screen appears. Tap OK to uninstall the app, or tap Cancel to keep the app.

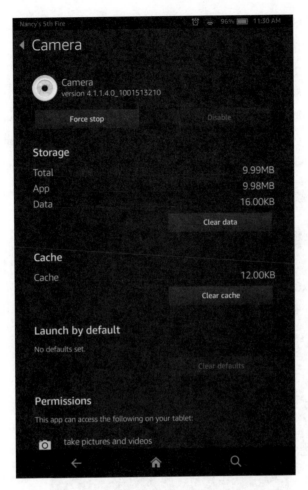

Figure 13-6: This app screen offers lots of information about the app's use of resources.

Viewing How Much Storage You Have Available

Fire tablets, like most tablets, have limited memory compared to your average computer. If you got one with very little storage, such as an 8GB 6- or 7-inch Fire, you'll quickly run out of storage. This can slow your tablet's performance or keep you from downloading any more content.

If either of these things happens, check to see how much storage is available and what's using your memory. Then you could uninstall memory-hogging content or apps you no longer need. (See the preceding section to discover how to uninstall an app.)

Follow these steps to check on your Fire's storage:

1. **Display the Quick Settings and then tap Settings.**

2. **Tap Device Options.**

3. **Tap Storage.**

   The Storage screen shown in Figure 13-7 appears. The colored bands in the Your Files display tell you, at a glance, which type of app or content is using up your storage space.

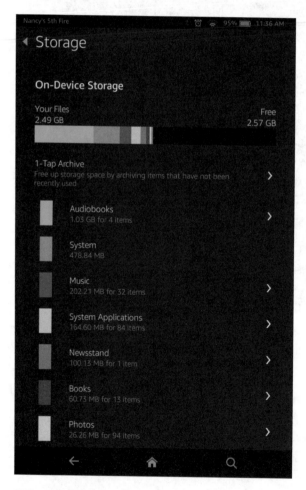

Figure 13-7: Study these colored bands to see what's eating up your memory.

4. **Tap a category such as Audiobooks or Applications to see which items in each category are taking up space.**

5. **Tap a check box next to an item and then tap the Remove button to remove it from your device.**

   You can also tap Clear All or Select All to take more global actions.

Remember, removing something from your device that you purchased from Amazon doesn't mean you can't access it in the Amazon Cloud or re-download it at a later time.

Closing All Tabs in Silk

If you sometimes get into long browsing sessions on your Fire tablet using the Silk browser, you can end up with lots of tabs open.

To get rid of the clutter, use this simple trick: With Silk open, press on any open tab. In the menu that appears, tap Close All Tabs (or tap Close Other Tabs to close all tabs but the one you're pressed). Simple!

Including Original Message Contents in an Email Reply

The eternal email quandary: whether to include a long string of replies when you respond to a message or to go with a cleaner look and lose the original message? Luckily, you have the power to choose your preferred style with Fire tablet email settings.

Perform these steps to include original contents in your email replies:

1. **Display the Quick Settings and then tap Settings.**

2. **Tap Applications.**

3. **Tap Email, Contacts, Calendar.**

4. **Tap Email Settings.**

5. **Tap the Off/On switch for the Include Original Message in Replies setting. See Figure 13-8.**

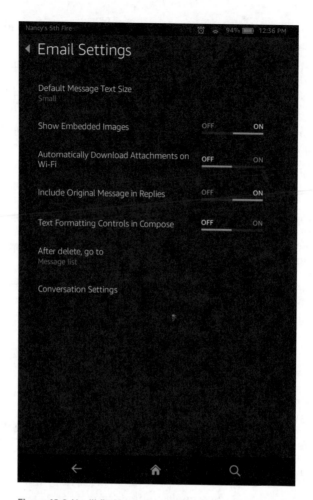

Figure 13-8: You'll find lots of handy email settings here.

Anytime you want to change this setting, just repeat these steps. You might also explore a few other email settings here, such as turning on text-formatting tools when composing a message. These settings can make the Email app work the way you prefer.

14

Ten (or so) Great Fire Apps

In This Chapter

▶ Writing and drawing with your Fire tablet

▶ Going by the numbers

▶ Tracking your investments

▶ Playing games

Any mobile device today, from a smartphone to a tablet, depends on the thousands of apps that make a world of features available.

Your Fire tablet has functionality built in for consuming books, periodicals, music, and video, as well as a contact management and calendar app, web browser, calendar, clock, and email client. However, some tools are missing. You can easily acquire this functionality by adding apps to the device.

Amazon Appstore, whose ins and outs you can read about in Chapter 6, contains thousands of cool apps for you to explore. From a very cool drawing app to a handful of games, the apps I describe in this chapter provide you fun and useful functionality for your Fire tablet, and they won't cost you much more than the time to download them.

In this chapter, I introduce you to 11 great apps that could create the core of a great Fire app library.

Sketch Book Mobile

From: AutoDesk, Inc.

Price: $1.99

Sketch Book (see Figure 14-1) is a drawing app to satisfy the creative artist in your soul. With dozens of preset brushes, you can draw whatever you can imagine on your Fire screen. You can control the brush characteristics and make use of an extensive color palette.

Try *sideloading* (transferring from your computer via a cable) or taking photos with your Fire and modifying them with this clever app, then saving your files in JPEG, PNG, or PSD formats. When you're done, it's easy to email your artistic efforts to yourself to print from your computer.

The Brush Properties' circular control lets you easily adjust the size and *opacity* (transparency) of the writing tools. The red arrow lets you delete the last lines that you drew, while the green arrow lets you add the deleted lines back in. When you pinch your fingers to reduce the scale of the picture, or expand your fingers to increase the scale of the picture, a handy feature shows you the percent of change. You can move your drawing around the screen and control the darkness and lightness of the lines in your drawing.

For a different art app, you can try Sketch n Draw Pad HD (free) or have fun with Drawdle ($0.99), a self-professed "drawing-based physics puzzle game."

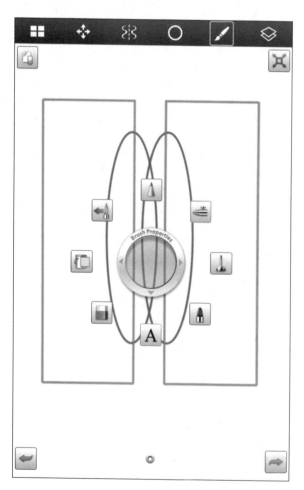

Figure 14-1: Sketch Book brings out the artist in you.

Family Budget Count Free

From: Astral Web, Inc.

Price: Free

If you're like many of us, these days, you're tightening your belt and counting those pennies. Family Budget is an app that helps you keep track of all your expenses, whether for a single trip or your yearly household budget. You can enter earnings and use built-in categories for fixed expenditures to categorize your expenses.

You can control your expenditures by day, month, or year (see Figure 14-2). You can also add notes to your expenses and check your budget balance easily.

Figure 14-2: Use various tools to enter and visualize your spending practices.

Bloomberg

From: Bloomberg L.P.

Price: Free

If investing is your thing, you'll find this stock reporting and tracking tool incredibly useful. The information is up to the minute and features both stock quotes and financial news. You can find updates on equity, commodity, bond, and currency market activity, as well as industry data and stock prices.

You can create a portfolio of your investments to help you track them more easily, and even watch videos about top financial news stories right on your Fire tablet.

All in all you can get a very comprehensive picture of what is driving current financial conditions, all from within this one app (see Figure 14-3). Check out the Exclusive list to read stories from Bloomberg's own insightful editors.

Convertr

From: Vervv LLC

Price: $1.99

If, like me, you need help converting just about anything to anything else (feet to meters, pounds to kilos, or whatever), you'll appreciate this handy little app with a clean, uncluttered interface (see Figure 14-4). Here are the things you can convert using this app:

- Angle
- Area
- Currency
- Data Rate
- Data Size
- Density
- Energy
- Force
- Frequency (disabled by default)
- Fuel
- Length

- Mass and Weight
- Power
- Pressure
- Speed
- Temperature
- Time
- Torque
- Typography
- Volume

Figure 14-3: Get a good feel for finances with Bloomberg.

Figure 14-4: Convert temperature scales easily.

If you're scientifically minded, you'll be glad to know that you can get your conversion to up to 12 decimal points. Each conversion category has multiple options; for example, the Length category has 13 conversion units and Volume has 15. Convertr updates currency prices constantly.

Wifi Analyzer

From: farproc

Price: Free

Because Wi-Fi–only Fire tablets can connect to the web only through Wi-Fi, this handy app is helpful for keeping track of local Wi-Fi connections. You can observe available Wi-Fi channels and the signal strength on each (see Figure 14-5). There are several styles of graph to choose from, including Channel, Time, Channel Rating, and Signal Meter.

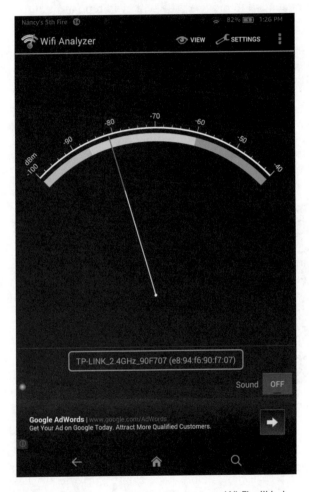

Figure 14-5: Figure out whether your nearest Wi-Fi will help you connect.

Contre Jour

From: Chillingo

Price: $1.99

This game has been called the intellectual's Cut the Rope because it uses the same premise of swinging a creature around a space to land on the winning spot, but in a much more sophisticated environment (see Figure 14-6). Against its black-and-white abstract art background that would warm Salvador Dali's heart, you're challenged to move a little one-eyed blob around to collect bits of light.

The game involves prodding the landscape to reshape it and thereby roll or push the creature toward the lights. There are also tentacles that you can use to latch onto the creature and swing it toward the lights.

To complete the game, your little blob must hit the big ball of light. Remember to collect other bits of light along the way to rack up higher scores. A lovely little piece of music plays in the background, but you can turn it off when you inevitably get tired of it. This is a fun, mentally challenging, one-person game worth checking out.

Figure 14-6: Use what's at hand to send your blob into the light.

Where's My Perry?

From: Disney

Price: $2.99

Based on the cartoon character Perry the Platypus, otherwise known as Agent P, this game is probably my favorite of the bunch. Perry is trapped underground in a little glass cage and you have to set him free (see Figure 14-7). To do that, you release water, steam, or ice to direct water into the pipe leading to his chamber. You can slide your finger across the screen to dig tunnels and direct materials into pipes.

Figure 14-7: Help Perry escape his cage with the power of water.

However, along the way you'll encounter lots of interesting variations. Sometimes you release steam to trigger a mechanism that opens a gate and allows water to come through. Sometimes you have to figure out how to melt ice into water with a laser. Don't forget to whack as many gnomes as you can along the way to score enough points to move to the next level.

Figuring out how to free Perry each time takes real problem-solving skills and makes for a game that challenges your brain. Despite the Disney connection, this one is great for kids and adults.

Stray Souls: Dollhouse Story

From: Alawar Entertainment

Price: $2.99

This is your typical, creepy-old-house, found-objects game, and it's a very well-executed one at that. Two newlyweds are at home one evening when a knock comes on the door. A package has been left on the doorstep and the husband instantly disappears. The game involves the wife looking for clues to where he might have gone.

As you move around to different locations (like the one shown in Figure 14-8), looking for clues, you have to pick up items such as pliers to open the package and a key to unlock a drawer. You pick up items like a torn photo and have to search for the other half. The music is appropriately creepy, and the "plot" is clever.

You can get hints if you are stuck, and there's a strategy guide for each chapter of play. You can also choose your level of play: casual or expert.

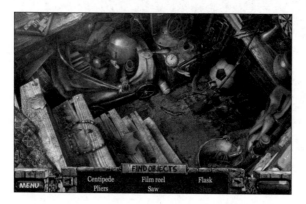

Figure 14-8: Solve the mystery by accumulating objects.

Chess Free

From: Optime Software

Price: Free

If chess is your thing, you'll enjoy this electronic version. You can play the computer or play against another person using the same Fire tablet. With the latter approach, the board swaps around after each play so that the next person can take his or her turn. There's a game timer if you're in Chess Tournament mode. You can also change the style of the pieces and board.

Tap a piece, and then the game shows you all possible moves unless you turn off Show Legal and Last Moves in the game's Options. Tap the place on the board where you want to move the piece (see Figure 14-9). In case you have a change of heart, this game includes a handy Undo button.

Figure 14-9: If you love chess, try out this version.

Solitaire Free Pack

From: Tesseract Mobile Software

Price: Free

This game doesn't have too many surprises, but for those who are devoted to solitaire, it offers an electronic version that you can play on the go on your Fire (see Figure 14-10). Rack up the points with 50 different games, including Klondike, Pyramid, and Monte Carlo.

Figure 14-10: If you're alone, try a round of solitaire.

You can change the card backgrounds and track your game scores to see whether you're improving as you go. If you want, you can take advantage of the unlimited redo feature to try and try again to win a game.

Real Racing 3

From: Electronic Arts, Inc.

Price: Free

If you love to race fast cars, this game will give you that experience on your Fire tablet with sharp graphics and quick moves. You can play around with more than 900 racing events with any of 22 vehicles in a wide variety of settings (see Figure 14-11). You can play locally on your Fire or with others in the app's Time Shifted Multiplayer technology.

Figure 14-11: Do you fancy a Bugatti, a Porsche, or a Lamborghini? They're all available here to test drive on tracks from around the world.

Beware: This game has drop-dead gorgeous graphics, but the trade-off is that you'll eat up a big chunk of your device's storage when you download it.

Note that with your Fire tablet, you get an accelerometer, gyroscope, and Adreno 330 GPU (graphics processing unit), all technobabble for features that let action games live large. Think tilting your Fire to move around the streets of Tokyo in a race car or shaking up your onscreen world in a battle between titans. Trust me, it's cool.

Be sure to check out GameCircle, Amazon's new combination of social networking and gaming. Open the Games library and tap the Left Nav button and then tap GameCircle Games. Buy one of these games (many are free) and you can then share scores, achievements, and the games that you love to play with others.

Index

About the Author

Nancy Muir is the author/co-author of more than 100 books on topics ranging from Internet safety and nanotechnology to a variety of computer and software topics. She has won awards from the Independent Booksellers Association and The Society for Technical Communication. Her experience includes working for and consulting with several major publishers on book series and strategies, as well as working in the software industry as a training manager. Nancy holds a Certificate in Distance Learning Design from the University of Washington.

Dedication

To my Uncle Ted, who is missed, and my Aunt Joan who will always be treasured.

Author's Acknowledgments

Thanks to Katie Mohr, the best darn acquisitions editor in the world, for all her support and efforts on this book. Thanks also to Tonya Cupp for steering the editorial ship and getting us into port. My tech editor, Earl Boysen, made the whole crazy process of writing this book on an aggressive schedule bearable and provided excellent input.

Publisher's Acknowledgments

Senior Acquisitions Editor: Katie Mohr

Project Editor: Tonya Maddox Cupp

Technical Editor: Earl Boysen

Editorial Assistant: Claire Brock

Sr. Editorial Assistant: Cherie Case

Project Coordinator: Patrick Redmond

Project Manager: Mary Corder

Cover Image: © Nancy Muir